THE SOCIAL
ADVISOR

SOCIAL MEDIA SECRETS OF
THE FINANCIAL INDUSTRY

amy mcilwain

WITH AMY NICOLE SMITH

Cover and interior design by Katie Malone.

ISBN-13: 978-1479196517
ISBN-10: 1479196517

DEDICATION

For Financial Social Media,

An amazing team without whom this
would never have been possible. Thank you for
continually pushing the envelope and inspiring me
to be the best that I can be.

TABLE OF CONTENTS

PREFACE

INTRODUCTION

"All lasting business is built on friendship"
—Alfred A. Montapert

Back in college, there was a coffee shop that I religiously visited called Common Grounds. It wasn't a large or particularly flashy establishment. In fact, the poor ventilation, local elementary school paintings, and cracked brick walls gave it an archaic feel. While it was what some would consider a "hole in the wall," I developed an unforgettable relationship with the small venue.

In fact, I'll never forget the first time I set foot into Common Grounds. As a new resident of a large city, I thought *what the heck, I'll give it a try.* On a crisp Sunday morning, I visited the shop for the first time. Upon opening the creaky door, I was greeted with a genuine smile from the barista. Before proceeding to ask what I wanted, she asked me how my day was going—a simple, yet powerful gesture that sparked a nice conversation about my studies and future plans. Her sincere customer service made a strong first impression—causing me to come back a second time, and continuously for the subsequent years. Every time I visited the coffee shop, I was addressed by my first name and rarely had to order my beverage—as they already knew what I wanted. On many occasions, they even gave me drinks for free. Their humility, care, and ability to listen made me feel like I was more than a customer—it made me feel like I was a friend.

That small hole-in-the-wall shop etched its way into my college experience, and I will probably always think of it while recounting old memories. At that time, social media didn't exist, but if it did, Common Grounds could have built an online empire with their old-school, above-and-beyond, relationship-building approach to business.

In today's increasingly robotic, cutthroat business climate, it's rare to experience the quality, relationship-oriented customer service that places like Common Grounds perfected. Nowadays when I visit a coffee shop, I receive a quality product, but I feel like somewhat of a "means to an end", rather than a valued member of a community. This experience isn't unique to my location—all across the board, quality customer service is frequently lost in the shadow of generating profits.

In the book *Enchantment: The Art of Changing Hearts, Minds, and Actions*, Guy Kawasaki brilliantly states, "When you enchant people, your goal is not to make money or get them to do what you want, but to fill them with great delight." Although social media is new and somewhat intimidating, it offers the quintessential vehicle to re-kindle the old school, tried-and-true business methods that don't simply "satisfy" your clients, but "enchant" them. With the right mindset, knowledge, and tools, you, as financial professionals, have the power to etch your way into people's cherished life memories, like Common Grounds did with me.

CHAPTER 1

SOCIAL MEDIA: THE NEW MEDIUM FOR CONNECTION

"In a chronically leaking boat, energy devoted to changing vessels is more productive than energy devoted to patching leaks." -Warren Buffett

Communication is weaved into the very fabric of the human code. Whether it is hieroglyphics, instant messaging, sign language, non-verbal gestures, or "liking" something on Facebook—we all communicate and have a keen desire to be heard. Years ago, I read a book by psychologist Marshall Rosenberg that provided a comprehensive list of human needs, built on the findings of extensive psychological research. According to Rosenberg, the seven umbrella human needs are connection, physical well-being, honesty, play, peace, autonomy, and meaning. Among the seven, *connection* and *meaning* were the two largest categories. Furthermore, in Maslow's Hierarchy of Needs Study, it is suggested that after the essential needs of survival and security, the greatest human need is to be accepted.

Those two studies single-handedly explain the explosive popularity of social media—as it satiates our deepest, most primal desire for connection, meaning, and acceptance. When you wipe away the technical jibber jabber, social jargon, and fancy designs—all that remains is a new medium for fulfilling the timeless human needs. If you approach it with this perspective, you're already on the path to success.

What is Social Media?

So we know that social media is a big deal, but what exactly is it? For the sake of formality, I will provide a concise, yet encompassing definition of social media. The best, most simple version I've read is as follows: "social media are technologies used to turn communication into interactive dialogue between organizations, communities, and individuals." But I'd be selling you short if I left it at that.

Social Media is...a level playing field. Nowadays, regardless of your marketing budget or business size, your message has the power to reach more people than you can imagine. With social media, the playing field is level—your voice is no more powerful or weak than anybody else's.

Social Media is...communication without borders. At any given moment, millions of people around the world are on social media connecting, doing business, exchanging experiences, making recommendations, and communicating without borders. Fifty years ago, it was challenging to share your message with a handful of people; now you can send it to millions with the simple click of a button.

*Social Media is…*word of mouth on steroids. Instead of rummaging through advertisements, consumer reports and product reviews, prospects and leads log onto Facebook, Twitter, and YouTube to gain perspective on products and services and are seeking the opinions of their peers. Research suggests that as a financial advisor, 100 people will visit your website before they ever set foot in your office. If you are a business with clients, you can bet your marbles that people are talking about you online.

*Social Media is…*the power of the people. With nearly a billion minds, eyes, and ears on social networks, it is now possible for Joe Smith to bring big corporate conglomerates to their proverbial knees. Last year, a situation occurred when an employee of United Airlines damaged the Taylor guitar of one of their customers. After the incident, the customer confronted the airline service asking to be compensated for the damaged guitar. United failed to address the situation, so the angry customer proceeded to make a YouTube video about how the airline "breaks people's guitars." The video was and still is a viral sensation with over 11,000,000 views. After the video went viral, United of course attempted to compensate the customer in exchange to remove the video—but it was too late. Taylor guitars beat United to the punch—providing the man with several free guitars if he kept the video up (because it promoted their brand).

Don't believe me? Check out the video:
http://www.youtube.com/watch?v=5YGc4zOqozo

*Social Media is…*marketing at its finest. Imagine if 10 years ago you read a fortune cookie that said—"you will soon have the budget and means to build a brilliant marketing campaign that will be aimed at your exact target audience, build your brand, and cost virtually nothing." You would've laughed. But the fortune wouldn't have been lying. With social media, you have the ability to do all of those things. The first step is simply believing in its power and having the initiative to jump in and commit.

Social Media from a Bird's Eye View

Now that we've seen social media up close, let's take a few steps back to glance at it from a bird's eye view. At this point in time, 2012, there are five social platforms leading the industry. Take note—*at this specific moment in time.* If you fast forward two years from now you will probably read this section with a nostalgic chuckle, much like we do with black and white television, cassette tapes, and dial-up internet. But for learning's sake, here is a brief glimpse of the leaders.

Facebook
Facebook is the "the pub" of social media, because it's where people openly share the details of their life and you cannot predict whose two cents you'll hear next. With nearly one billion subscribers, if Facebook were a country it would be the world's third largest, trailing only behind China and India. Within the next twenty minutes, nearly 2 million photos and statuses will be updated, and there will be over 10 million comments made. And the numbers are growing at rates no business or website has ever seen.

Twitter
Twitter is frequently called the "cocktail party" of social media. If you've ever logged onto the platform, you know exactly why. At every moment of every day, millions of people are posting 140-character tweets, or short blurbs. Like a cocktail party, everyone talks or "tweets" at once. The appeal of Twitter is that it's always "in the moment"—meaning that people have instant access to the latest news and happenings—nothing more, nothing less. Prior to this network, it was nearly impossible to have your own news and radio station—now you can blast out your message to millions of

people in the blink of an eye. According to Twitter, more than 1 billion tweets will be sent this week.

LinkedIn
LinkedIn is often referred to as the "golf course" of social media. When compared to the other major social platforms, it possesses a high degree of formality and professionalism. Here, people aggregate to network, join industry groups, and participate in professional conversations. With over 170 million users, this platform not only bolsters your professional footprint, but it also opens you up to a world of information and opportunities pertaining to your business and professional life.

YouTube
I like to call YouTube the "Hollywood" of the social networks because it is your in-home recording studio and vehicle to stardom. Owned by Google, this platform is for original content creators and people all across the globe to connect, inform, and inspire others via short videos. There are hundreds of millions of people watching videos online daily. In fact, more content is uploaded to YouTube in a 60 day period than the three major U.S. television networks have created in the last 60 years. With YouTube, nearly a billion people across the globe have access to your voice—a staggering reality that has unlimited potential for you and your business.

Pinterest
Although numbers indicate that Pinterest lags behind Twitter, Facebook, and LinkedIn—its roaring popularity is truly a force to be reckoned with. Reaching a predominantly female demographic, Pinterest is on the cutting-edge of creative social media platforms. Comprised of virtual pinboards, it allows users to keep track of their favorite things—such as recipes, sports gear, blog posts, financial resources, fashion, and more. While at first glance it may seems like this platform is solely for crafty soccer moms in mini-vans, it should not

stray far from your radar. It offers the opportunity to not only promote your brand in a creative way, but also to pioneer the female demographic.

With millions of participants and users across the planet, social media is re-shaping the way we, as humans, communicate. From small, interpersonal interactions to presidential elections to nationwide revolutions, it's the new, powerful force molding our history as we speak.

The Power of Social Media

November 5th, 2008 is a day that will forever be ingrained in our nation's history. Millions of Americans gazed at television screens, gathered in the streets, and stood in emotional awe as Barack Obama won the 2008 presidential election. The live television coverage, montages of photos, collections of articles, and ocean of "Change" logos only capture a small fraction of the unforgettable day.

Not only was Obama the first African-American president in the history of the United States—he also defied all odds to reach his success. In 2004, he could have walked down any street without receiving a second glance by a passerby. But within 4 short years he became a household name and assumed the role as one of the most powerful individuals in the United States. How did this happen?

Obama entered the election with a keen awareness that his funds were limited compared to those of his opponents. Consequently, he geared his electoral campaign away from dominating traditional media (newspapers, television, radio). Instead he harnessed the unforeseen power of a new medium—social media—to not only raise funds, but connect with the influential 18-29 year-old demographic.

By election day, it was clear that his strategy flourished. He not only fundraised $500 million, but a staggering 23 million 18 to 29 year-olds showed up at the polls, the majority supporting him. While there were a number of factors that contributed to his success, like his gift for oratory, the social media numbers tell a story of their own. Here is a snapshot of Obama's and McCain's social footprints on Election Day.

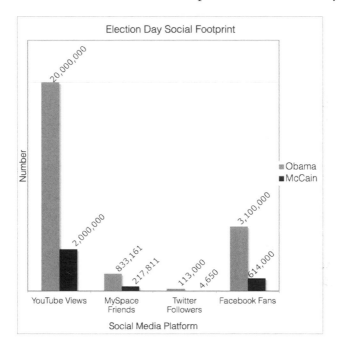

The 2008 election is only one of many powerful occasions where social media played a quintessential role. In the years to come, I see social media as being the epicenter of not only presidential elections, but marketing campaigns, causes, protests, and movements all across the globe. If a relatively unknown politician can rise to stardom and win an election within 4 years, there is no reason why your business cannot achieve ground-breaking results with social media too.

Social Media and Financial Professionals

Now that you've (hopefully) grasped the meteoric influence and power of social media, it's time to assess what it means to *you* as a financial professional. Given the highly regulated nature of the financial services industry, it's easy to understand why financial professionals are hesitant and apathetic towards social media. Beyond the regulations and compliance concerns (which we address in chapter 9),

> *"Failure is not fatal, but failure to not change might be."*
>
> -John Wooden

there are a host of misconceptions about social media preventing financial professionals from proactive embracement. After consulting a wide range of clients and gaining over a decade of experience in the industry, I have a pretty solid grasp of the most common myths and fear factors associated with social media. Here are the top six.

The Top Six Social Media Myths [Debunked]

6 My Audience is Not on Social Media

At speaking engagements, I always tell the all-too-familiar story of my mother, the stereotypically baby boomer. Years ago, she used to confidently proclaim, "Oh, I'll never text message—that's for young people." Now, I frequently receive text AND picture messages from her. She also used to say, "Oh Facebook, that's for the kids." I'm sure you can guess how that story ends.

• **Young high-net worth (HNW) individuals:** A recent study from the Federal Reserve's Board of Consumer Finances claims that "high-net worth individuals under the age of 50 hold 28% of the US wealth across all asset classes." It goes without question that these waves of young HNW individuals are accustomed and comfortable with new social technologies. A 2011 Spectrum Group

Study also reveals that "younger investors are likely to view a financial advisor in a negative light if he/she does not have a social media presence." Knowing this, it is important to anticipate a growth in young HNW individuals and a widespread transfer of wealth from baby boomers to the more tech-savvy Gen X and Gen Y.

• **Investors exchange information online:** Apart from a way to exchange information, social media is increasingly influencing investors' decisions. According to the Cisco IBSG report (2011), investors exchange information and guide each other on blogs and message boards. Furthermore, many young HNW individuals use social media channels to converse about investment decisions.

• **The percentage of baby boomers using social media is consistently growing:** According to a study from the Pew Internet & American Life Project, the use of social networks by people ages 50+ has grown over 40% in the past 7 years. This illustrates that the older generations are slowly (but surely) adopting and using social media. AARP also cites that in the United States, there is an estimated 270 million internet users and one-third of them are from the baby boomer generation — which means you're looking at more than 80 million baby boomers that are using social media.

#5 It's Unprofessional

If social media were unprofessional, professional corporations, individuals, and businesses would not be utilizing it. Social Media Today posits that over two-thirds of Fortune 500 companies are on social media, including giants like Verizon, Coca-Cola, Best Buy, Southwest Airlines, and Starbucks. If the most brilliant and successful business leaders in America are hopping on the social bandwagon, it's a good indicator that it is in fact professional.

#4 I'll Never Gain the Support of My Firm

Dwight Eisenhower once said, "Leadership [is] the art of getting someone else to do something you want done because he wants to do it." Once you clearly understand the potential power of social media, it will become easier to convey the benefits to the higher-ups. Among an array of benefits, it reduces marketing costs, improves client relationships, increases referrals, and helps you establish yourself as a trustworthy expert in your field. As you learn more about social media, the undeniable benefits naturally emerge.

#3 There's No Way to Adhere to Compliance Policies

According to many studies and surveys, compliance issues are the primary chains holding back the use of social media in the financial industry. Almost three-fourths of financial advisors say their firms have a written policy about using social media. Of them, 82% say the policy limits or prohibits use. While strict regulations are admittedly suffocating, they mustn't shield the vast reservoir of growth lying before your business. There are myriad social media compliance products for business professionals. The key is gaining a thorough understanding of the regulations set forth by FINRA, the SEC, and the NAIC regarding social media. From there, you can begin to develop compliant systems and processes that work.

#2 It's a Huge Time Sucker

I hear this one a lot. Let's face it: social media initially takes time—but with solid systems and processes in place, your social media operation will run like a well-oiled machine. There is also a conglomeration of available tools to shorten the process and have scheduled and automated output.

It's important to remember, however, that social media is personal and "in the moment." Your audience will really appreciate seeing real, genuine posts from your business, for they are interested in *you* more than anything. How do you save time and increase efficiency with social media? Check out some of the top social media time savers at the end of this chapter.

#1 It's a Fad

Because social media is still an infant in the technological world, many skeptics still dismiss the phenomenon as a "fad," like a fuel-lit fire that explodes and quickly fades. If you've been in the business long enough you may recall when email was first introduced in the late 1990's. Many thought email was a fad. Could you imagine where your business would be today if you hadn't adapted to email? Communication is shifting again. And it's happening twice as fast.

Warren Buffet once said "in a chronically leaking boat, energy devoted to changing vessels is more productive than energy devoted to patching the leaks." This couldn't be more true. What worked 10 years ago doesn't work anymore. The boat is sinking. You cannot keep throwing more money at the same things over and over again, because it's not going to fix anything. It's time to change vessels—and the new vessel is the internet. Mark Matson of Matson Money recently made a prediction that "only 15% of current advisors will be left within the next 5 years." Do you want to be one of the 15%? Or do you want to sink with the ship?

SOCIAL MEDIA TIME SAVERS

Create pre-packaged posts: Spend a chunk of time creating a collection of pre-packaged posts, pictures, quotes, and article links that you can pull from when you're really busy. Here at Financial Social Media, we like to create a library of quotes and posts to draw from when we need fast content.

Use social media aggregation tools: There are a medley of great social aggregation platforms to schedule content for all of your social platforms in one easy place. Tweet Deck and HootSuite are among our list of favorites. Sign up and save hours of time.

Create an editorial calendar: Editorial calendars are an awesome way to map out your entire social media marketing strategy. They not only help you strategize your content, they also promote continuity between different social platforms and ensure that everyone (associates, guest contributors, ect.) is on the same page.

Hire an intern or delegate responsibility: Social media should be a collaborative effort. If you're the only one managing the social media operations, you might consider rotating the responsibility between others in the office. As long as your brand's voice is consistent, this is a great way to keep ideas fresh and evenly distribute the load.

Guest contributors: Having guest contributors—especially when it comes to your blog—is an incredible time saver. Not only that, but it keeps your blog fresh with creative voices. Find a list of people and publications that you can exchange content with. Chances are they're scrambling for content too, so it'll be a great opportunity to build a mutually beneficial relationship rooted in sharing content.

Use your phone: We all have times when we're waiting in the grocery line or at the DMV—use these opportunities to post to your social networks from your smartphone. Who says you can't kill two birds with one stone?

RSS feeds: RSS stands for Really Simple Syndication and it is a great way to keep a constant stream of posts on your platforms. Because it's automated, you don't have to worry about posting or visiting the website. To set it up, all you have to do is visit a website/publication and select an RSS feed that parallels the interests/needs of your target audience. From there you can select how often you'd like the feed to appear on your platforms.

Google Alerts: Google Alerts are e-mail updates of the latest relevant Google results (web, news, etc.) based on your queries. All you have to do is enter a search query you wish to monitor and select how often you'd like to receive updates. Google Alerts are great for monitoring a developing news story and keeping current on competitor or industry trends—all of which are great springboards for blogs, videos, tweets, and Facebook posts.

Personalized content: So you can't seem to find and/or develop interesting content today? Try taking a step outside of the norm and posting something personal, such as pictures from your last vacation, your daughter's graduation, or your latest speaking engagement. There is nothing wrong with sprinkling personal touches onto your social platforms. As financial advisors, this is a great way to save time and build trust with clients, leads, and prospects.

Daily Checklist: Financial Social Media's Daily Checklist offers some great routines and guidelines for daily posting on your social networks. It not only takes away the think-work associated with posting and engaging, it also teaches you a great deal about how and when to engage. To view the Daily Checklist, visit the Resources section in the back of this book.

CHAPTER 2

THE AGE OF CONTENT MARKETING

_____

"Man cannot discover new oceans unless he has the courage to lose sight of the shore." -Andre Gide

Imagine you're driving home from a long, stressful day at the office. Not only are you drowning in deadlines, but you have yet to organize the messy compilation of documents in your briefcase and desk at home. On the long stretch of highway, you see a billboard out of the corner of your eye with a huge logo and tagline promoting an office supply store. You cast a glance at the billboard, have a fleeting thought about the image, and drive on without another thought about it.

After arriving home, you have a few hours to kill before your kids get home from football practice, so you get online to look for quick organization tips. You come across an interesting blog by another office supply company—"10 Office Organization Tips that Will Change Your Life." You skim the blog and gain valuable insights about how to effectively organize your office. Because of this great piece of content, you subscribe to the blog and refer back to it again and again for organization tips. A month goes by and you finally find the time to make a purchase on office supplies. Which company do you think will be at the top of your mind?

The difference between traditional marketing and social media marketing is the difference between *saying* you're a valuable company and *showing* you're a valuable company. In this digital age, consumers are increasingly desensitized to jingles, billboards, and television commercials, which present static messages without the opportunity for dialogue. Social media and online marketing, on the other hand, allow for a continuous business to business and/or business to consumer conversation. When a message or idea is presented, the conversation doesn't end—it only begins. While there is still a place for traditional marketing, social media marketing offers incredible opportunities to build valuable, genuine, and long lasting relationships with existing and potential clients via *conversations*.

If I could give advisors one piece of advice, it would be to be authentic. There is nothing more important than your social media voice reflecting who you really are as a person and as a professional. Part of the divide between the public and financial services industry is this notion that there is so much phony bologna going on. So if your social media messaging is thick with BS it is almost more apparent than being full of it at a networking function. Be who you are and if you don't think people will like who you are then figure that out before you get on social media.

-Stephanie Holmes
@TheMoneyFinder

CHAPTER 2

Old School Practices, New School Mediums

"You can make more friends in two months by becoming interested in other people than you can in two years by trying to get other people interested in you"
-Dale Carnegie

When you strip away the colors, flashy applications, and cutting-edge platforms, social media is simply relationship building. It's not much different than attending networking events, trade conferences or impromptu coffee dates with prospects. The only difference is the medium. Dale Carnegie's 1936 book *How to Win Friends and Influence People* offers timeless strategies for building relationships, getting people to adopt your way of thinking, and gaining leadership. Although the book was written 80 years ago, long preceding the birth of social media, it is applicable in our contemporary world of virtual "likes," "friends," and "fans." Why? Because effective human relations skills are the timeless crux of building successful businesses and relationships. Jot down, highlight, and laminate these rules as you embark on your social media quest, for they won't lead you astray.

Become Genuinely Interested in Other People
Have you ever met people who talk and/or post solely about themselves? It might look like this: "here's a picture of my lunch, I'm feeling pretty blue today, I'm going to the baseball game tonight." Me, me, me, me! Here's the deal: everyone wants to talk about themselves. The key is striking a balance between talking about yourself and engaging with others. With social media, you can do this by asking questions to your audience, posting material that is of keen interest to them, and starting discussions that are on the forefront of their mind. Here are some examples of how you can express interest in others:

- What is your dream retirement location?
- We are having a financial workshop at XYZ restaurant. Where do you dine most frequently?
- The guest speaker on today's webinar is a local CPA. Who would you like to hear from next week?

Be a Good Listener and Encourage Others to Talk About Themselves

This aligns with the notion of becoming genuinely interested in others. But it goes further by saying "be a good *listener"* and *"encourage others to talk about themselves."* You cannot build strong relationships without listening skills—especially in the financial services industry. Listening also involves engaging and prompting people to talk about what matters to them. Here are a few ways you can do this on social media:

- "Like" and comment on other peoples' posts. Perhaps comment with a question.
- Ask questions and conduct polls.
- On Twitter, @mention people to start discussions and share interesting material.
- If others send you messages, post about you, or tweet about you, *always* listen and respond accordingly.

Talk in Terms of Other People's Interests

I am an avid runner. And while I could talk all day and all night about trails, upcoming races, and the latest shoe releases —not all people can relate. It's great to talk about your passions and personal interests, but you'll attract more people by talking in terms of their interests. On social media, do this by:

- Finding out what's interesting to your audience. Is it golf? Is it top retirement locations? Is it fine wine? Constantly strategize about how you can feed your audience's interests.

- Discover what's going on in the lives of your audience. Are they approaching retirement? Preparing to send their kids to college? Learning to invest?
- What are some of the problems your audience faces? Talking in terms of other people's interests also involves talking about the problems and worries they face. In other words, *what keeps them up at night?* By addressing these concerns and worries via blog and social media posts, you will begin capturing the trust and respect of your audience.

Make a Person Feel Important, and Do It Sincerely
By following the latter rules proposed by Carnegie, you will naturally make your digital followers and friends feel important. You can also make others feel important by:

- Engaging with their material via comments, likes, and shares
- Acknowledging the comments and likes you receive
- Offering kind words frequently
- Answering questions and concerns within a reasonable time frame

When I initially launched my company, Financial Social Media, I was adamant about building my brand and positioning myself as the authority on social media in the financial services industry. One strategy to accomplish this goal was getting my content published in national financial publications. For those of you who have dabbled in PR, you know how difficult it can be to grab the attention of editors and decision makers.

Being the nature of my business, I turned to social media to tackle this endeavor by following many of the publications and thought leaders on Twitter and Facebook. I also did a little digging, acquired the names of the specific editors I needed to contact, and connected with them on Twitter and

LinkedIn. When I was in their realm of sight, I began consistently writing comments on their blogs, "liking" their posts on Facebook, and re-tweeting their content. By engaging and showing interest on their networks, they started taking notice in my brand. As a result, I've since had several articles published in prominent national magazines and have become a regular contributor to several financial blogs and newsletters. You can do the same in your local area! You are an expert in your field. Position yourself as such and have your voice heard.

Give Honest and Sincere Appreciation
People long to feel indispensable and appreciated. By offering small tokens of gratitude, you'll go a long way in getting people to like and trust you. On social media, this often takes the form of thanking people for their engagement and/or their business. I do this a lot with clients, prospects, and those I want to develop strategic partnerships with.

> Social Media Secret: Create reminders of clients' milestones, such as birthdays, one year business anniversaries, ect. and engage with them on Twitter and Facebook on those days.

4 Technologies that went from Old-School to New-School

From Paper Invitations to Evites
Before the birth of the internet, we sent invitations via the post office. While mail is not quite obsolete, there are some amazing new ways to invite and attract people to your events via social media. On Facebook, you can create event pages and invite specific people to join. The same goes for LinkedIn. These tools are great because you can easily follow up with people you invited and continually promote the event until it occurs.

From Photo Albums to Online Albums

Images are integral to the human experience. I'm sure we can agree that there's a universal and captivating element about taking and viewing pictures. With social media, you can upload photos within minutes and instantly capture the attention of your followers.

From In-Person Meetings to Virtual Meetings

Instead of scheduling conferences, meetings, and dates, it is now possible to have virtual, face-to-face meetings with people online. With interfaces like Skype, video conferencing, and Google Hangouts, you can chat with your co-workers, clients, family, and friends with the fast click of a button.

From Day Planners to Virtual Planners

When I was in school, I used day planners and agendas to schedule my deadlines and appointments. Now, with the creation of new scheduling technologies, it is possible to create online calendars that do the organization for you. With platforms like Google Calendars and SalesForce, it is possible to easily sync your calendar with others and with other technologies like smartphones. You can also set up alerts and reminders to keep you organized all day long.

It goes without question that technology is changing at a rapid rate. While the bells and whistles may seem a bit intimidating, it's important to remember that new technologies are simply new mediums for achieving the foundational principles of human communication and connection.

> We're all talking about this like it's optional. It's not. If you're a financial advisor and you meet a Gen Y guy at a party, a 30-year-old who's making some real money, and he goes to look you up on Google and doesn't find you, to him you don't exist. This is not optional.
>
> -Josh Brown,
> @ReformedBroker

CHAPTER 3

DEVELOPING A STRONG CONTENT AND SOCIAL MEDIA STRATEGY

"Traditional marketing talks at people.
Content marketing talks with them." —Doug Kessler

The Four E's of Content Marketing

Instead of being static, content marketing is interactive and conversational. After working with hundreds of financial advisors, we've been able to identify the four most powerful elements of content marketing:

Educate

With blogs and social media, you have the power to position yourself as an expert in your field with a variety of mediums. For example, with your blog you can produce educational content that aligns with your services and piques the interest of your target audience. On Twitter, you can keep your audience up to date on breaking news and the "here and now." On YouTube, you can upload videos with information about the most pressing financial questions. Regardless of the interface, brainstorm how you can educate your audience.

Prominent media spokesperson Mark Matson of Matson Money started out his media appearances with his MarkMatson.TV network. Now, he not only continues to use this platform as a megaphone to deliver his message, but he is also continually featured on national syndications such as CNBC "Kudlow Report" and "Power Lunch," Fox Business News "Opening Bell," "Power and Money" and "Closing Bell," and CNBC Reports.

Empower
Traditional marketing mediums like magazine articles, billboards, and television commercials pump people with information but fail to empower people to grow and evolve. With content marketing, your business has the opportunity to empower people with the information, insights, and resources they need to be truly successful in their financial lives. This may come in the form of financial calculators, educational webinars, coaching calls, podcasts, or videos. But more simply, it consists of offering legendary customer service. If you haven't already, you will soon learn that people are using social media to ask questions and address concerns. By being available on social networks, you will be ten steps ahead of the game when it comes to customer service.

Entertain

Another key element of content and social media marketing is to branch out and have fun! Many advisors fail to understand and embrace the light-hearted, entertaining nature of social media. It's not all about black and white, cut and dry business marketing. You can branch out and post jokes, quotes, images, videos, factoids, and questions to drive engagement with your audience. As long as it aligns with your goals and business expertise, it's a wise idea to seek ways to entertain.

Engage

Engagement is the key element that separates traditional marketing from content marketing. Static marketing (like billboards and brochures) leaves no room for conversation; content and social media marketing *is* a conversation. By posting blogs, Facebook statuses, tweets, videos, and content on LinkedIn, you are setting the stage for important conversations. Unlike any form of advertising, you can engage, build trust, and foster brand loyalty with the mere click of a button.

How to Develop a Social Media Strategy

Establish Goals

In *Digital Leader*, Erik Qualman states, "Having a huge goal inspires us mentally and physically to overcome the hurdles and obstacles that we will encounter along the path. People should laugh at the audacity of our goals... A good understanding of what you want most in life will separate you from

99 percent of the crowd." The heart of any great social media strategy is a keen understanding of what your firm's strengths, weaknesses, and goals are. Like a high school fashion fad, many companies jump on the social bandwagon because they think it's what they *should* do or because *it's what everyone else is doing.* But before you dive into social media you must first establish your goals and understand what you are trying to achieve. If you don't know where you are going, how do you know when you have arrived? Setting goals will also help you to monitor and adjust your campaign as you move forward.

If you cannot pinpoint exactly what your goals are--take a few steps back to establish them. Here are some common online marketing goals that advisors set:

- Improved customer service
- Leads
- Improved SEO
- Increased web traffic
- Brand awareness
- Increased revenue
- Client retention
- Faster closing
- Decreased marketing expenses
- Increased customer referrals
- Increased partnerships

Organize and Plan
"Stop thinking campaigns. Start thinking conversations." You might be thinking, "social media and blogs aren't my forte, I'm a financial advisor, and don't have time for all of this." I completely agree, which is why you need to create a plan to ensure social media operations run smoothly and efficiently. To get started, I recommend creating an editorial calendar.

Many people connote editorial calendars with big, fancy magazine or print publications. But you can rest assured that they aren't complicated, or even fancy. They are simply a medium for controlling the publication of content across different media, like blogs, email newsletters, and social media outlets like Twitter and Facebook fan pages.

Here are some of the top reasons to adopt this strategy:

- **A plan:** So you and other contributors can stay on the same page and plan ahead. With the use of an editorial calendar you can manage your blog in a way that several different contributing writers can view their future topic, and plan for when it will be due.

- **Cohesiveness:** It allows you to cater all of your social media posts to specific topics or ideas. For example, it is great for ensuring that there is cohesiveness between your Twitter, Facebook, and blog posts.

- **Time:** It saves a ton of time. Our thoughts are often fragmented and unorganized, but the editorial calendar lets you plot those ideas into meaningful content that can be expressed in a timely manner. Having an editorial calendar allows you to delegate your limited cognitive energy to different tasks.

- **Trial and error:** It helps you keep track of what works and doesn't work. With monitoring tools, you can look back and see when you had the most traffic/engagement.

- **Strategy:** It helps you develop strategies around specific holidays, company events, or cultural occasions.

Editorial calendars can be as specific or as broad as you want. They can cover all your social media accounts, or just one. It can be a yearly calendar with monthly themes, or a monthly calendar with weekly themes. It can be available to just a few others involved, or to a wide range of contributors and users.

The bottom line is that the editorial calendars are whatever you *need* them be. Here are some tips to get the ball rolling:

- **Decide which platforms your calendar will include:** Does your editorial calendar include your blog—or does it include other social platforms such as Facebook and Twitter? You may want to create a calendar for each platform, but it's important that there is consistency and cohesiveness between them.

- **Create a list of SEO keywords:** SEO stands for Search Engine Optimization. In a nutshell, you should develop a strong list of keywords associated with your business and continually reuse them on your on your blog, website, and social media platforms. These words will not only help you rank higher on Google and other search engines, they will also improve your search rankings on each individual social platform. Example: If you are an RIA in Broomfield, Colorado, who specializes in retirement planning and college investment planning—you will want to constantly re-use words such as RIA, Broomfield, retirement planning, and college planning on your online marketing platforms. That way, if someone searches "Retirement Planning Broomfield" on LinkedIn, you will be one of the first visible profiles.

- **Aim at your target audience:** The next step is to determine who you want to attract to your blogs and pages and how you plan to attract them. This can start broad but you want to narrow it down as much as you can. The more specific your target audience, the easier it is to create content that will hit the bull's-eye. Think back to the old 20/80 rule: what 20% of your clients account for 80% of your revenue? Yes, I'm sure a lot of you would like to reach people nearing retirement with more than a million dollars in investable income. But what do they have in common? Do they collect antique automobiles? Enjoy golf? Look beyond the surface and dig down into your target audience's hobbies, education level, socioeconomic status, career, gender, etc. Remember at the beginning when I said the way to get people to come back to your social media platforms is to give them what they want? Well here is when you figure out exactly what it is that they want. Speak their language, understand their needs, and be aware of the hot, trending topics in their world.

- **Create a master list of topics:** Once you determine your audience, you can create your topic list. This is the step that saves you from those writer's block moments. The list should match your firm's key areas of expertise to your audience's key areas of interest and need. These topics can serve as an idea bank for future blog posts and content planning as well as serve as a basis for new topics to arise. I suggest brainstorming at least 5 to 10 of your firm's key areas of expertise and services, such as retirement planning, estate planning, investing, or insurance. Use these topics as springboards for social media and blog posts. And as a friendly reminder, don't ever seek to self-promote or explicitly advertise your business via blogs and social media. As a content producer, you're here to create content that benefits, educates, and provokes thought for your audience.

- **Deadlines and publishing days:** Choose specific days when blog and social media posts are due for edits, and days when they go live each week. Here at Financial Social Media, we post blogs on Tuesday's and Thursday's because that's what works best for our team and has proven to be most viewed by our audience. Select deadlines that are convenient for you, your writers, and your readers. When inviting guest authors, make sure you give them at least 2 to 3 weeks to write the post—assuming they are very busy and that there will be edits.

- **Themes:** There are several ways to approach themes. Some people like to create recurring weekly themes like "Retirement Tuesday" or "Money Saver Monday;" others like to establish monthly themes like "April: Taxes" and "August: Planning for Education." When it comes to developing themes, do what works best for you and your staff. The important key is keeping content fresh and relevant.

  The College Funding Connection has a "Financial Aid Question of the Month."

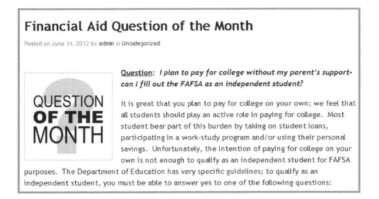

Financial Aid Question of the Month

Posted on June 14, 2012 by admin in Uncategorized

QUESTION OF THE MONTH

Question: *I plan to pay for college without my parent's support- can I fill out the FAFSA as an independent student?*

It is great that you plan to pay for college on your own; we feel that all students should play an active role in paying for college. Most student bear part of this burden by taking on student loans, participating in a work-study program and/or using their personal savings. Unfortunately, the intention of paying for college on your own is not enough to qualify as an independent student for FAFSA purposes. The Department of Education has very specific guidelines; to qualify as an independent student, you must be able to answer yes to one of the following questions:

- **Holidays/current events:** Take into consideration holidays, cultural traditions, current events, and milestones. Perhaps you might cater your content to the Super Bowl, The Olympic Games, or the Fourth of July. Regardless of which ones you choose, remember to creatively tie it back into your field. The Retirement Guys, Nolan Baker and Mark Clair, provide an excellent example of this with their Fourth of July themed post titled "Why Our Heros Die" where they talk about the concept of freedom and their mission of helping people become financially self-reliant.

- **Mediums:** Many financial professionals still think that all blog content has to be produced by themselves or their team. This couldn't be further from the truth. There are a plethora of styles and strategies for producing content. It doesn't always have to be a cut-and-dry informative piece. Schedule variety in your social media and blog calendar— such as how-to's, case studies, opinion pieces, interviews, guest blog contributions, insightful pieces, testimonials, podcasts, videos, commentaries, and more.

Defining Success with ROI and KPI

Think back to the last time you attended a trade conference, a chamber networking event, or an impromptu coffee meeting with a lead. During these occasions, I assume you engaged in conversation, exchanged pleasantries, passed out business cards, and gave brilliant elevator speeches. In other words, you "spread the seeds" of your business with hopes that some would grow into lasting business relationships.

Let's face it, many seeds whittled and faded; but others probably developed into fruitful returns on your investment of time and energy.

Similar to relationship building meetings and events, social media offers the platforms to spread the seeds of your business to the world. Measuring the growth of the seeds, however, can be a challenging concept to grasp, but it begins by shifting your definition of your return on investment (ROI) and developing a solid list of key performance indicators (KPI). Below are three indispensable strategies to consider when it comes to measuring social media ROI.

(1) Change Your Perspective: Back in the day (1990's), it was easy to launch a marketing campaign and measure the success via bottom line growth. With social media marketing, it's a little different. Many advisors (understandably) struggle grasping the benefits and potential returns of social media. With a little shift in perspective, however, the benefits and/or returns are hard to ignore.

"Do not go where the path may lead; go instead where there is not path and leave a trail."

-Ralph Waldo Emerson

- **Cost savings:** Let me state the obvious: social media is cheap and in many cases free. By having stellar social media processes and operations, you will save your company a boatload of money that otherwise would be spent on costly marketing campaigns. Don't ignore this when examining benefits and returns.

- **Search engine rankings:** Google is the #1 search engine tool in the world and is an integral part of many people's' day-to-day lives. Think of social media as the vehicle to increased search engine rankings and ultimately worldwide exposure.

- **Cost avoidance:** If you've accepted it or not, people are talking about your business on social media. Whether or not you choose to participate in this conversation is up to you. I don't know about you, but if I knew people were talking about me in real life, I'd want to be there to save face. On social media, you have the power to not only listen in, but monitor the conversations that are buzzing about your business. Just think—putting an end to one negative conversation may result in one new client that may have never looked twice.

- **Sales and revenue:** Just because the "bottom line" is no longer the only measure of success, it should be ignored. Continue to measure the relationship between your business' bottom line and your social media efforts. Still shaking your head? Check out this success story:

David Armstrong, Wealth Manager from LPL, wins a $3M account from a prospect who followed his firm's Facebook Page for 8 months. Armstrong was prospecting an owner of a small business, who wasn't ready to make a decision at the time. The small business owner did however decide to follow him on Facebook. Eight months later, the prospect told him, "I love what you have been writing for the last eight months. I'm ready to move my accounts with you". Armstrong's story serves as a powerful example of how financial professionals can get huge returns using social media.

- **Social capital:** Social capital refers to the collective or economic benefits of knowing people. In other words, the more people you know, the more likely you are to gain referrals and prospects, get preferential treatment, and develop your "celebrity" so to speak.

(2) Keep track of the seeds that grow with KPI: Key Performance Indicators are the mediums through which your business assesses success. I cannot emphasize enough the importance of measuring your performance. You'll waste years of time and energy if you fail to do so. Here's how you can get started:

- **Create categories:** Choose metrics that you can translate into business categories, such as sales, leads, customer satisfaction, customer interaction, etc. Determine these categories based on the goals of your business. For example, if you're seeking to increase referrals, use referrals as a unit of measurement.

- **Stop fixating on your "likes":** Define more than just "attention" metrics (# of followers, etc). For financial professionals, it takes time to develop a large following. And, while it's great to have as many followers as possible, it's essential to expand your attention to other areas such as higher search engine rankings, follower engagement (likes, comments, shares), and weekly total reach.

- **KPI's for each social network:** Each social network is different. On Facebook you may measure your "weekly total reach" whereas on YouTube you may measure the # of video views. Regardless, make sure you cater KPI's to the specific network.

(3) Check out some Monitoring Gems: Below are some awesome, free tools to help you gauge the performance of your social media marketing. The information and insights you obtain from these sources will be useful in all realms of your business.

- **Facebook Insights:** Facebook Insights is a great tool to measure the impact of your posts, how many people are talking about your page, demographics, and your weekly total reach outside of your fanbase. You can access insights by logging into your business page and clicking on the admin panel.

- **Google Analytics (free):** With Google Analytics, you can insert a line of code into your website and keep track of how people get to your site, how they navigate through it, and how long they stay.

- **YouTube channel stats:** On YouTube, you can keep track of video views, demographics, playback locations, traffic sources, audience retention, subscribers, views and more.

- **Going Up!:** This is another free web analytics package that helps you monitor traffic trends, SEO, keywords, and user profile data.

- **LinkedIn:** LinkedIn is not necessarily a monitoring tool, but it can provide good information about your connections. Use it to keep track of what your competitors, industry trends, and hot discussions.

To sum it up, there really is no one universal understanding of "success" in the social media world. Rather, "success" is dependent on how you define it. Regardless of your goals, you must define success on a large scale (ROI), and then acquire small scale key performance indicators (KPI).

> *"[Social Media] is not an overnight pot of gold, but I think it's like email...eventually everyone will be using it. You don't want to be last. It's a very effective way to maintain contact with your clients and provide them with ways to refer you to their friends. You'll also be surprised how many old acquaintances will call you for help once they learn what you do. That said, it's important to be on the cutting edge: Update your website regularly, use video, learn what others are doing and try it yourself. Keep it fresh and people will keep reading your work."*
>
> -Dan Cuprill , The Angry Capitalist, @DanCuprill

CHAPTER 4

FACEBOOK: THE FACE OF SOCIAL MEDIA

"In the long history of humankind those who learned to collaborate and improvise most effectively have prevailed." -Charles Darwin

From Facemash to Internet Phenomenon

What is the first thing that pops into your mind when I say "social media?" If you're remotely familiar with what social media is, your first thought was probably Facebook.

What is now known as an internet empire was born in a small, rather insignificant dorm room at Harvard University. 20-year old, techie Mark Zuckerberg and three of his classmates developed an immature platform called Facemash, where students rated whether other Harvard students were "hot" or "not." According to the *The Harvard Crimson*, Facemash "used photos compiled from the online facebooks of nine houses, placing two next to each other at a time and asking users to choose the 'hotter' person."

After some less-than-ideal, and not-so-surprising reactions, Zuckerberg revamped his initial project by creating a social study tool before an art history final. He opened the site for classmates to exchange notes for the test. According to a TechCrunch interview, Zuckerberg claims, "The professor said it had the best grades of any final he'd ever given. This was my first social hack. With Facebook, I wanted to make something that would make Harvard more open."

Five years and several lawsuits later, the site went from Facemash to thefacebook to just "Facebook." In 2005, the site extended to several other Ivy League schools and in 2012, nearly ten years after the birth of the offensive "hot" or "not" platform, the phenomenon now known as Facebook has weaved its way into the very fabric of cultures across the globe.

Facebook is now literally the "face" of social media. On Facebook, people from every corner and crevice of the planet connect, share their lives, and have dynamic interactions with friends, celebrities, businesses, bands, organizations, causes, and much, much more. With nearly 1 billion users, if Facebook were a country, it would be the third largest, trailing only behind India and China. Within the next decade, it isn't absurd to assume it'll leave those two countries in the dust.

In fact, Facebook is so widespread, that some psychiatrists and employers now find it suspicious for an individual to keep off Facebook, reports *The Daily Mail*. That's because in today's society, having Facebook is considered "normal," while opting out is considered "abnormal" and may suggest that an individual may have something to hide by not participating.

No More Excuses!

We're at a point in history where the world is at our fingertips. With the mere click of a button or a touch of a screen, we can access anything our mind can conceive—people, knowledge, places, businesses—you name it. The technological developments in the past decade have not only reshaped the way we, as humans, interact and communicate—they have also reshaped the way business is conducted.

It goes without question that Facebook is the social media giant of our time. It is perhaps the most popular, groundbreaking, and influential platform the world has ever seen—connecting nearly 1 billion people across the globe. At no other point in history have this many people been connected on one single online platform. If your business isn't a part of this vast global community, you're literally tossing one of the most powerful components of growth and success out the window.

Perhaps you view Facebook as a personal platform and feel skeptical about connecting with clients. I get it. In fact, when it comes to social media marketing, Facebook was one of the *last* channels I dove into for business purposes. To me it was too transparent. I didn't want clients seeing the same pictures and posts as my college buddies, or worse—having a friend post an embarrassing comment on my page! However, I've come to realize that whether we like it or not, the openness of social media means it's almost impossible to keep different parts of our lives distinct. By avoiding Facebook, I was missing out on some incredible opportunities. If used properly, Facebook is the quintessential platform to build strong, lasting connections with clients, acquire leads, and increase referrals.

If you're not on Facebook, make a point to log onto face-book.com today to set up a personal account. It's not only simple and user-friendly, but it's the best, most inexpensive vehicle for promoting your brand to millions of people.

The Scoop on Personal and Business Pages

These days, one of the first places people go to checkout your business is Facebook. Believe it or not, if you don't have a page established, it causes your business to lose credibility.

So what's the difference between a profile and a fan page? Think of facebook like a giant shopping mall with almost 1 billion people. You, as an individual, are represented by a profile, while your fan page is your business' storefront in this shopping mall. Let's face it: your clients are there, your prospects are there, and your business needs to be there as well.

Fan pages also allow you to keep your business and personal life separate inside of the Facebook realm because your profile and your business' fan page are two completely different entities. Someone who "likes" your fan page doesn't gain access to your profile, and anything that you post to your personal profile doesn't get updated to all the fans of your business. This setup gives users the separability they want between their personal lives and their business lives on Facebook by giving them the best of both worlds.

Setting Expectations

High five! You've set up a personal and business fan page! But before you kick back and indulge in a glass of Chateau Haut-Brion, you need to brace yourself because the fun has only begun. Your Facebook page will be useless if your timeline is blank and your following number has a big fat "0." Here are two virtues to embrace when you start working on Facebook:

Patience

Contrary to popular thought--the Facebook world won't stop in its tracks once your business page is up and running. There are millions of businesses competing for your audience's attention, and you need to differentiate yourself from the crowd. As explained in chapter 3, there are several steps you must take to be successful: set goals, organize and plan, and then define success and establish key performance indicators. Keep in mind that it takes about six months to start seeing results, so strive to remain persistent and optimistic. Here are some ways to ensure you're maximizing your time and increasing efficiency:

- Keep track of your results. Learn what drives engagement and what doesn't.
- Be creative. Experiment with different types of content to see what gets the most feedback.
- Cross promote. Promote your Facebook page on your website, blog, and other social media accounts. On Facebook, you can access free social plugins, such as a "like" button, that you can embed on other networks.

Diligence

Have you ever visited a ghost town? Vacant buildings, weeds, broken windows, abandoned sheds. Not only are they creepy, but they're extremely unattractive. I'm willing to bet that you've never sought to re-visit any ghost

"I average 30-45 minutes a day on social media per week, but I don't hold to a specific time per day. I can tell you every second I've turned into an investment and I've seen fabulous returns on Facebook."

-Stephanie Holmes, @TheMoneyFinder

town you've ever been to, right? Idle Facebook pages are just as unattractive as ghost towns. To be perfectly honest, they scream "I don't care!" Is that the message you want to send to a billion people? If you invested in a billboard, you wouldn't want it to be outdated or blank. The same rules apply here. Be diligent and consistent with posting and engaging no matter what! And remember: tis' better to have no Facebook page than an abandoned Facebook page. If time is really an issue, consider doing the following:

1. Delegate tasks to an intern or others in the office.
2. Sign up for RSS Feeds (really simple syndication).
3. Schedule posts on social media aggregation sites like HootSuite.
4. Follow an editorial calendar to help you develop ideas.

Now that you've set your expectations straight, let's dive into the fun stuff! Facebook allows you to connect and engage with consumers on a more personal level. Most Facebook users put their life out in the open because they want to share; they want to communicate with others; they want to foster valuable relationships. The same is true with your business. Ultimately people want to do business with other people who they know, like and trust. Facebook gives you the opportunity to share who you are and what makes your business tick. Ask yourself, why would someone want to be a fan of my business? Let's discuss the possible answers to this million-dollar question that will help you manage a successful Facebook fan page.

• **To receive valuable industry information:** Many fans of Facebook pages use their "likes" as a way to load their newsfeed with valuable information about a specific industry. Think of it as another version of an RSS feed – an investor will become a fan of multiple financial publications and organizations in order to receive up-to-date news and information on the financial industry. This means that your fan page needs to be pushing top notch information that's relevant to your fans and your industry. However, be careful of the frequency in which you post to your fan page – you do not want to overload your fans' newsfeeds, so think quality over quantity. As a financial professional, aim to post 1-3 times a day.

- **To receive company news and updates:** Some Facebook users have become fans of your page because they want to follow your business and receive company news and updates. These are the kinds of fans that either already have brand loyalty or are simply looking to learn more about your company. To fulfill your duties to these types of fans, make sure you're posting relevant and up to date company news, such as upcoming events, promotions and media appearances.

- **To become a brand ambassador:** These are the fans that business owners love. These types of fans already have loyalty to your brand and are looking to become a brand ambassador to help you spread the word. You're probably asking yourself, do I have these types of fans? Of course you do! These fans are your employees, friends, family members and current clients. They already know your business and are representing it in some way or another. The key is to push them to market your brand even more, so ask them to send out fan page invites to their friends. Ask them to post fan page information on their personal profiles. Brand ambassadors are there to represent your business and attract new fans.

- **To follow up on a promotional incentive:** These people have probably run across your fan page from a promotional incentive or through another user's newsfeed. The first step is to get them to click "like." Creating a reveal page that incentivizes them to click "like" in order to see specific content is a great strategy. Try hosting a video or special promotion to entice non-fans to click "like." You also have a tough job in front of you in order to keep those fans. In order to do that, look back to answers 1 and 2 – continue to push out relevant industry news and keep your fans updated on company updates.

One of the biggest challenges with any social network is to get followers to interact and engage with the company. The key to a conversation is a two-way street of interaction, so make sure you're doing your part to add value to discussions and page communications. Social media is all about relationships, but if there is no commitment from both parties you'll fail to see your networks grow.

Strategies for Facebook Success

With Facebook, there is no scientific formula for "success" for driving engagement and developing a robust following. But here are few fundamental guidelines to consider to get you off on the right foot:

Establish your Brand
Having brand consistency is extremely important. Graphics, colors, voice, verbiage, and overall feel should be parallel across all online channels. Just think: Who are you? What do you stand for? What makes you different than every other advisor out there? What message do you want to be sending to your clients and prospects?

Determine your Audience
In order to promote your brand to the right people, you need to determine who your audience is. Think of the 80/20 rule again. What 20% of your clients make up 80% of your business? What do they have in common? What is their age, oc-

cupation, gender, hobbies, etc? What are they already buying? What do you want to offer them? What is their online behavior and tone? How do they like to be engaged? If you don't know who you are talking to, you won't know what to say. You want your message to be targeted each and every time you post, share and comment.

Build Your Audience
Once you have your foundations in place, you can begin the fun part: building your audience! Nothing compares to the warm fuzzies you get when someone "likes" your page. Here are some ways to boost your following:

- **Cross promote across networks:** This is such a simple practice. If you acquire a following on Twitter or LinkedIn, ask them check out your Facebook page too.

- **Widgets:** Widgets are those cool pictures you can embed on your website, blog, and newsletters that prompt people to "like" you or visit your Facebook page. You can access these directly from your Facebook page.

- **Invite your friends:** You have the option to invite all of your personal friends to  "like" your business page. From my experience, this is an effective kick-starter for getting more fans.

- **Use Facebook Ads:** Facebook Ads are an amazing feature on Facebook. For a minimal price, you can develop advertisements that target specific audiences, such as 50 to 65 year-old males who like golf that live in Wausau, Wisconsin. Or 50+ single women who may be recently divorced or

widowed. With Facebook Ads, businesses typically have a logo and a call to action, such as "Like" us or "Download our free investment guide." You also have the option to pay per click or pay per impression.

Driving Engagement

> "Don't be too personal or unprofessional. Try to remain unbiased and take the middle ground whenever possible and avoid commentary when can't be avoided. Remember in life only about 50% of the people will like you so play to those 50% and disregard as much as possible the other 50%. Do not think it will generate a path of new prospects to your door or website, it is just another inexpensive and awesome way to build and enhance credibility."
>
> -Michael Ham,
> @MyMoneyTrack

Driving engagement is one of the keys to success on Facebook. But in order to effectively do this, you need to create compelling content that piques and demands the interest of your audience. Here are some ideas:

Post Blogs
So you just posted a blog, "10 Interesting Facts about Long Term Care." Post this content to your Facebook wall with an engaging question: "What surprises you most about long term care?"

Share Articles by Others
Think of yourself as the "Content DJ" filtering through the barrage of content available online and sharing only the best and most relevant articles for your audience.

Ask Questions

This goes back to Carnegie's advice to "become genuinely interested in the other person." Asking questions drives engagement and shows that you're interested. They can be related to your industry or more generalized. Here are some examples:

- What is your greatest financial concern?
- What are you doing for Labor Day?
- Where do you want to retire?

Create Events

Do you have an upcoming seminar, client appreciation event, or speaking engagement coming up? Facebook is the perfect place to create events and promote them to your networks. I would suggest posting about the event before, during, and after it's complete. I also suggest taking lots of pictures and videos, directing attendees to your Facebook page, and posting them to Facebook after the event. People love seeing pictures of themselves, so this is an awesome way to drive traffic and foster engagement on your page.

Use Humor

A little humor goes a long way on Facebook. Consider posting funny and witty images, cartoons, videos, and quotes (within appropriate parameters, of course) to get a rise out of your audience. For example, Colorado's Citywide Banks posts a recurring theme of "Friday Funnies."

Videos

We will delve a little deeper into video in the YouTube chapter, but it's a great idea to post relevant, timely, and interesting videos on your page. Remember the four umbrella goals of empowering, educating, entertaining, and engaging.

Polls

Is there a hot topic that your audience is buzzing about? Create a poll to get their feedback!

Quotes

People love quotes. Create a library of interesting quotes to sprinkle into your posting schedule.

Ask for the "Like," "Share" or "Comment"

There are several studies that suggest that asking for the action increases engagement. So instead of simply posting an article, post the article and say "comment with your opinion on life insurance" or "click 'like' if you learned something."

Use Fill in the Blank Posts

"For the holiday weekend I'd like to _____."

Encourage "Check-Ins" at Your Location

When people "check-in" at your business, all of their friends see it. This is a great way to drive engagement and increase brand exposure.

Facebook's Secret Weapon: Targeted Advertising

Have you ever noticed the ads on the right side of your Facebook homepage? If not, go to your homepage and take a look. You may find yourself taking

"When we first created our fan-page, I took a shot at advertising by using the free $50 coupon FB sent. The traffic to our page more than doubled. For $10 a day, we made a good first impact and frankly, the time it would take me to get in front of all those new people is well worth the money. As a drip marketing technique, I think spending the $300 a month is something we will continue to do as we experiment with the types of content that people want to see."

– Chris Storace
@StoraceWealth

special interest in these ads. I bet it seems like they are directed to you and your interests, right? This is no accident.

The efficiency of Facebook Ads is made possible by Facbook's Reaching and Targeting Initiative, which captures specific profile information and ensures your ad reaches the right audience. Eureka! This means that Facebook, the social network giant, has given you the opportunity to advertise your brand to millions of consumers online with precise targeting.

In case you missed the memo, there are nearly 1 billion people worldwide on Facebook. Each month, those billions of connections form a digital map of people's real world networks of family, friends, co-workers, hobbies, and even products. For an advertiser, profile data is a gold mine for reaching customers. User profiles outline important demographics such as status updates, birthdays, occupations, hobbies, location, and relationship status. Because Facebook Ads can access this information, you can target the correct people.

As an advisor, are you looking to reach 55+ engineers who like to travel, play golf, and live within a 20-mile radius? How about 45 to 55 year-old single women who need financial advice? Facebook can put your targeted message in front of these people! It eliminates the guessing games and puts an end to wasting money on reaching the wrong audience.

If you are still hesitant about Facebook, revert back to one of the most basic principles of marketing: go where your audience is. And trust me, your audience *is* on Facebook and will continue to be for the years to come. This opportunity is way too good to pass up, so get started!

5 Step Guide to Advertising on Facebook

Step 1: Choose what to promote: What do you want to promote? Do you want to promote your page, event, app or a website outside of Facebook?

If you decide to promote your Page, you can take several routes. You can promote:
- A new ad about your Page
- A post on your Page
- When people "like" your Page
- When people "like" your Page post

If you want to drive more traffic to your website, consider promoting your brand with a link to your webpage and/or Facebook page. You may also consider promoting an important event or article. Regardless of what you decide to do, make sure your ad aligns with your marketing goals.

Step 2: Target the Right People: Who is your target? Think about the profiles (timelines) of the people you want to reach with your ads, and select criteria based on what your audience is interested in, instead of what they might be looking to buy.

With Facebook Ads you can target by:
- Language, Location, Work, and Education
- Age, Gender, Birthday, and Relationship Status
- Likes & Interests: Select Likes & Interests such as "golf", "church", or "travel" instead of "the Bible" or "golf clubs"
- Friends of Connections
- Connections

When you select a criterion, you will be given an "estimated reach" which tells you exactly how many people, within your demographics, will potentially see your ad. If you have the goal of reaching a broad, widespread audience, aim to have a higher estimated reach number. If your goal is to get a more localized return, aim for a more narrow reach.

Step 3: Design your Ad: Just like any form of advertising, trial and error is inevitable. Create multiple versions of your ads with different images and body copy to find out which combinations are most effective. Here are some tips for creating effective ads:

- Include your business or Page name, a question, or key information in the title
- Provide a clear call to action and highlight the benefits (not features) of your brand
- Use a simple, eye-catching image that is related to your body copy and title
- Target different audiences to determine which groups are most responsive to your ads

Step 4: Budgeting: With Facebook ads, you have several budget options:

- CPC vs. CPM: You can pay a cost-per-click (CPC), where you get charged when people click on your ad or a cost per thousand impressions (CPM) where there is a cost per 1,000 times your ad or is displayed. Whether you choose the CPC or CPM option depends on your goals. For example, if you want to increase brand exposure, you should select the CPM option. If you want to increase "likes" or traffic to your page, you should select the CPC option.
- Daily Budget: Set the maximum amount you want to pay each day – once you hit your daily budget your ad will no longer show. For example, if you set a $5 per day limit and you select a CPC option with each click being 50 cents, then your ad will no longer show once you get 10 clicks on the ad.
- **Bid Price:** Bid prices fluctuate. Set a bid with the suggested range, and check your Ads Manager often to update it when the suggested range changes

Step 5: Metrics: After you launch your ads, you can check out detailed metrics and reports to help you improve your performance. Continue to check your Ads Manager after you launch your campaigns to create, edit, and optimize them. With your ads manager, you can:

- Get basic data about your ads, such as impressions and clicks
- Learn about your audience's age, gender, and location at an aggregate level—this can be great
- View specific time periods to learn how your ad performance has evolved

CHAPTER 5

BLOGGING

---

*"No matter what, the very first piece
of social media real estate I'd start
with is a blog" -Chris Brogan*

Blogging is a tool that has fallen within certain connotations over the years because it often serves as a platform for people to spout off their opinions about anything under the sun. Despite the bad rap, blogs are often much more than the culmination of gossipy posts. Wikipedia defines blogging as a "discussion or information site published on the World Wide Web consisting of discrete entries ("posts") typically displayed in reverse chronological order." This "discussion or information" is the valuable offering that will drive people to your site and, if you use it correctly, will keep them coming back.

Until 2009, blogging was typically the work of a single individual or small group and was often themed around a specific topic (like kayaking, running, or culinary arts). Now, however, blogging is an important ingredient to any business' online presence. One of the best examples of a blog's capability is Mashable. This blog was started in 2005, by a then 19-year-old Pete Cashmore, publishing up-to-the-minute news on social networks and digital trends. Now Mashable is heralded as one of the top ten most profitable blogs in the world and has proven to be worth hundreds of millions of dollars to CNN who has been in talks to purchase the company. The power of blogging is due to the vast array of purposes it can serve. Blogging is essential for:

- **Positioning yourself as an expert in your field:** By producing great content, you have the opportunity to make yourself the "go-to" in your industry. Let's assume Sally is interested in learning more about annuities. She begins her research online, and soon finds the information about annuities on your blog very helpful. Sally will have already built trust with your brand without even stepping foot in your office. These online interactions plant the seeds of opportunity.

- **Starting discussions and driving engagement:** In this information age, people aren't enticed by jingles, billboards, and sales pitches. They want value. By developing a blog, you are giving your readers (ahem, prospects!) content that is valuable to them. Imagine you are a single parent trying to save for your daughter's college education. Would you be enticed by a pop-up ad that said: "Joe Simmonds: The #1 College Advisor in Los Angeles" or a blog entitled, "10 Ways to Invest in your Child's College Education." Blogging gives you the opportunity to *show* you are an expert, not just *say* you are an expert. It also provides an opportunity to learn about your audience by observing what drives more traffic and engagement.

- **To improve your search engine rankings:** Remember the SEO keywords we discussed through setup and strategy? Your blog is a great place to sprinkle keywords to increase its search engine ranking.

- **Increasing exposure:** If you produce great content, people will circulate it, other bloggers will want you as a guest author, and media outlets will want to publish your content. Blogging is a great way to get major exposure and PR for your business. Did you know that when external sites link back to your site, it improves search engine rankings?

"I began blogging about a year ago and it has been the single best way to getting traffic to my website and top rankings with Google and Yahoo. I have not paid for any internet advertising or paid for Google Adwords or placement and yet my website www.mymoneytrack.com is the top listing for any combination of the words "Dallas personal budget or budgeting advice, help, assistance, counseling." I enjoy blogging and writing in general, to me its cathartic but if you're not much of a wordsmith, then again seek professional writers that can take you message and format it for the internet and attracting readership. Financial Social Media was the best at this, at least for me. Up to now, I have not purchased or had any SEO work performed for my website and yet the blogs still drive traffic."

-Michael Ham
@MyMoneyTrack

As you can see, there are some tremendous benefits to blogging. Let's discuss how you can get started.

Blog and Website: Your Online Bonnie and Clyde

A lot of people think "Well, I have a website. Why do I need a blog?" A blog and a website are not mutually exclusive tools, but rather work as a team to capture and foster an audience for your company. Your blog should be the heart of your website, constantly pumping out fresh, relevant content that will keep your visitors engaged. It acts as the beginning of the sales funnel bringing people into your website and opening them up to you, your business, your expertise and your services and like I said before, if you use it correctly, it will keep them coming back.

Your website should act as an online media hub, with outlets to all of your online information platforms. A social media optimized website should have four key components:

- Blog: The impetus behind people visiting and returning to your site.
- Lead Capture: To track the visitors of your page and gain valuable information into what they were looking at, for how long and when. This turns those visitors into tangible leads for your company.
- Social Media Icons: Displays your presence on social media and provides an outlet to your social media platforms.
- Social Media Widgets: These icons give little snippets of your social media platforms, such as your Twitter Feed or a "Like" button to engage users with your social media pages.

Having a blog is one thing, having it integrated into your website is another. As mentioned before, your blog and website work as a team, and having them separate of one another depletes their power. Linking to an outside page with your blog creates unnecessary friction for visitors on your site and frankly, they are less likely to make the jump and visit the separate page.

Another setback is that your website loses the powerful SEO perks that come with a blog. Your blog is a keyword honeypot for search engine optimization which can be a huge driver to your site, but without having your blog integrated, those SEO keywords won't be found in your website, so your website is less likely to be found by the millions of people using search engines to find sources.

The bottom line is this: your website needs to have a purpose. Whether that purpose is to provide information, generate leads, or sell a product, a blog can work to stimulate all of these. Your blog and website should be like Bonnie & Clyde-partners in crime. They each serve a valuable, reciprocal purpose in generating leads and closings.

In short, your website is the mousetrap and your blog is the cheese.

Blogging Strategies

Blogging is one of the keys to establishing yourself as reliable, high-quality expert in your field. The goal is to not explicitly proclaim the virtues of your products and services—like traditional marketing, but to communicate your expertise by creating content that is valuable to your target audience. Creating relevant content that strikes a deep chord with your audience inspires them to subscribe, share, and continually refer back to your platforms. If they trust you as a reliable and valuable source of information, it is likely that they'll be loyal to your brand. How can you create top-notch content? Here are some of the of golden nuggets of great blogging:

Images/ Photos

It goes without question that people love images. Just observe the top social media platforms like Facebook, Pinterest, and Google+. They are chock full of visual content! Photos drive engagement, "likes," shares, comments, and readership. Include pictures in your blogs. If you are not big on photography, you can purchase stock images, use free image hosting websites like www.morguefile.com, or take screenshots with free, downloadable software like Jing.

Awesome Headlines

Headlines may seem like a small detail, but it is unquestionable that a strong headline is a major factor in determining the success of your post. It can also be very challenging to come up with one! Here are some tips for creating shining, irresistible headlines:

- **"10 Best Cities to Retire In"**

  Strategy: Clear, concise, to the point; someone who reads this title knows exactly what to expect. It is straight to the point and gives the reader exactly what they are looking for.

- **"12 Must-Know Investing Strategies"**

  Strategy: Create a sense of urgency. You want people to think that they will be missing out on something critical if they don't drop what they are doing and read your article right now. You want to entice people and, in a way, make them afraid to miss out on your valuable information.

- **"How To Choose a Financial Advisor"**

  Strategy: "How-To's" are an amazing asset for title writing. Most people who are looking for information through a blog are wanting to know how to do something. A title like this tells them exactly what they will learn, and chances are, that is exactly what they are searching for.

- **"5 Biggest Mistakes to Avoid When Buying an Annuity"**

  Strategy: "How Not-To's" are just as great. As much as people want to know how to do something, they also want to know how to avoid screwing something up. Anyone who sees a title like this will check it out, if for nothing more than to see if they are committing one of those mistakes themselves.

- **"25 Ways to Save $100 Each Week"**

  Strategy: Numbering. You probably have seen something of a pattern developing on our examples so far: almost all of them use numbers. Numbers add a tangibility to the post that gives the reader an indication of what to expect. The more they know from the start, the more likely they will be to continue.

- **"Why Variable Annuities Suck"**

  Strategy: Be dramatic. If someone walks in and says "I had a bad day," and then someone else says "I've had the worst day ever!" whose story are you going to want to hear? Being a little sensational with your title draws the reader's attention and peaks their interest so that they can't help but want to know more. Even if this means being a little controversial or making a bold statement, don't hesitate to use it. Your title may coincide with or even contradict something that your reader believes, but either way they will have a hard time not checking it out.

- **"Startling Statistics on DIY Investors"**

  Strategy: Let them know you have data. As much as opinions and jazzy language have their place in blogs, people love cold hard facts. Hinting that you have new data or statistics that might surprise them is a great way to gain attention. Their subconscious will force them to read more.

- **"New Mutual Fund Changes Investing As We Know It"**

  Strategy: Make it a headline. If your post hits on new or groundbreaking content, make sure your readers know that from the start. By making the title relevant both in timeliness and newsworthiness it will give readers some motivation. Everyone wants to stay up with the times!

Keep It Conversational

Blogging is a unique genre of writing. Unfortunately, many people's experiences with writing is limited to essays in high school, technical writing, or proposals. Well gentlemen, loosen your ties; and ladies, let your hair down because blogging is less formal and more fun! Unlike other styles of writing, you can (and should!) be conversational, witty, opinionated, and creative. Interesting, conversational content generates more readership than heavy jargon. Just imagine: if you were learning about something that was foreign and

"I've noticed that when you tie in a personal story, you get a lot more interaction from the audience. I've also noticed that you get a lot of traction when you take a personal stance on an issue"

-Britney Castro,
Financially Wise Women,
@Brittneycastro

intimidating to you (like finances), you'd probably feel more engaged and comfortable reading a conversational, easy-to-digest article rather than something laden with words and ideas you *literally* have to translate.

Bullet Points or Numbers

As mentioned above, people like to know what to expect. They also like to skim. Given the plethora of information out there, it's better to make your blog as easy to navigate as possible. By incorporating bullet points and numbers into your articles, you make it easy for your audience to read, learn, and refer back to your content.

Links

Incorporate links throughout your blog--to statistics, other educational resources, or to your own website. It lends credibility and also makes your blog richer with resources and information. For example, if you reference an article or idea in your blog, provide a link back to the source or a place where the reader can acquire more information.

Stories and Imagery

Stories, legends, and myths are a universal human interest. Our lives are built--day in and day out--on stories. Trying to communicate an idea? Tell a simple story that illustrates your point. As long as it gracefully ties back into your topic, it is sure to pique your audience's interest. Also consider using words like "imagine" or "what if." Hypothetical situations prompt people to actively engage and critically think.

Take a Soap Box

Feel strongly about an issue? Your blog is a great place to voice your opinion. Unlike other forms of writing, it's perfectly acceptable, and often wise to be a little controversial on your blog. As always, make sure the content correlates with your business and is relevant to your audience. For example, a blogger at Financial Social Media recently came across an article that denounced the importance of social media for financial professionals. She quickly wrote an "in response to" piece that reversed the article's claims. This was a strategic and creative way to take a soap box and quickly spread via Facebook and Twitter.

Informative
People love stats, numbers, figures, and case studies. In terms of rhetoric, it appeals to the logical side of our mind that craves solid facts. If you're writing a piece on long term care, use a statistic like, "The lifetime probability of becoming disabled in at least two activities of daily living or of being cognitively impaired is 68% for people age 65 and older."

Educational
"How To's," "step by step guides," and "what to do if's" are great ways to generate interest. Let's face it, there is a lot of information and misinformation when it comes to financial matters. Educating your audience aligns with the goal of empowering your audience. As previously mentioned, aim to be the "go-to" in your field.

- What to do if your parents need long-term care
- How to determine which insurance is best for you

Video
When it comes to creating videos, there are some key strategies to embrace. According to Brent Coker, a marketing professor, the four key elements required for a video to go viral are:

- Congruency: The themes of a video must be congruent with people's pre-existing knowledge of the brand it is advertising.
- Emotive strength: Creating strong emotions is essential if you want to ensure you are giving your video

the best chance of becoming viral and the more extreme the emotions, the better.

- Network involvement: Videos must be relevant to a large network of people and the larger the better, some examples of large networks are college students or office workers.
- "Paired meme synergy": These memes can be elements such as "Voyeur" or "Unexpectedness." Check out some of these video blogs by financial advisors. When you create your videos, aim to deviate from the norm and engage your audience in unique ways.

Ed Slott, Stay Rich Tax Advisor, and Mark Matson, CEO and Founder of Matson Money, are the cream of the crop when it comes to video blogs—definitely check them out to get more ideas.

Going Live

Once your brilliant, innovative blog is complete, it's time to go live. There's more to going live than merely clicking "publish." In fact, you should set up a posting process that sets your content up for success.

Embedding on LinkedIn/Facebook
Downloading specific applications allows you to showcase your blog directly within your Facebook fan page and your Twitter profile.

Including Your Blog in Status Updates
Include your blog on all of your social media platforms and use compelling language to entice readers.

Twitter

On Twitter, post an enticing teaser with a link to your blog. If you want to target specific people and/or organizations, consider @mentioning them with the link to the blog. We'll go over this strategy more in the Twitter chapter.

Posting on Reader Forums

If you are a part of any forums, like Brightscope, FiPath or Tippybob, make sure to post your content there.

Share with Groups and Send Announcements on LinkedIn

There are a lot of awesome ways to circulate content on LinkedIn. Two strategies that I recommend are posting to groups and sending an announcement to your group members (if you host a group). Again, we'll touch on this more when we discuss LinkedIn.

You have spent time and energy creating a great blog with great content, do yourself a favor and put it in front of as many people as you can. Use the various outlets and resources available through your social media efforts to expand your audience and readership.

Generating PR with Your Blog

Blogs are an incredible way to generate exposure for your business. In fact, you *should* aim to get PR and media exposure with your content. Getting exposure from the media can be a huge asset for lead generation and lending credibility about your business.

Pitching Your Blogs to the Media

When pitching content to the media, you want to be concise, direct, and powerful. Publishers are very busy and are always on the hunt for content. By pitching quality, relevant content to them, you are essentially helping them. But to get in the door, you have to be very strategic in how you pitch. Follow the Ready, Aim, Fire method to get started:

- **Ready:** Research top industry publications where prospects and industry leaders are already at and where your content will get traction. Once you have a list of prospective publications, find out their information--specifically their e-mail addresses, blogs, LinkedIn accounts, and Twitter handles.

- **Aim:** Attack your publications and prospects from all angles. Follow them on Twitter, connect with them on LinkedIn, "like" them on Facebook, etc. Once you do this, start engaging with their content: comment on their LinkedIn posts, "like" their Facebook statuses, re-tweet their content, and comment on their blogs. This may seem silly, but it's a smart way to get your brand in front of your targets. Just think: if a company followed you on Twitter, connected with you on LinkedIn, "liked" you on Facebook, commented on your blog, and consistently engaged with your posts--you'd develop familiarity with that brand. This is exactly what you need to do with your target publications.

- **Fire:** Now that you've positioned yourself in front of your targets, it's time to contact them directly via e-mail. My suggestion is to create an e-mail template that you can reuse over and over. Here are a few things to consider while pitching to the media via e-mail:

  - Introduce yourself
  - Share a little information about your company
  - Establish credibility and highlight your expertise
  - Send samples of your content
  - Ask for the call!

Here is an Example:

Hi Bill,

My name is Rob Parker and I am the President and CEO at Parker Financial Group. I am an avid reader of the your online publication, Financial Today, specifically the Annuities Newsletter that comes out every Wednesday. I am very interested in the prospect of contributing to your publication and/or e-newsletter. Each week, we publish 2 blogs--one on annuities and one on retirement.

Here's a bit more about Rob Parker and our firm
Company: Parker Financial Group (link to website)
Author Bio: www.robparker.com

Parker Financial Group is committed to helping clients achieve financial peace and prosperity. Specializing in retirement planning, annuities, estate planning, and long term care--we're devoted to offering customized solutions that meet your individual needs.

We've had content published in (provide links)

- *Publication 1*
- *Publication 2*
- *Publication 3*
- *Publication 4*
- *More...*

Here are a few examples of our work:

- *Sample 1*
- *Sample 2*
- *Sample 3*
- *Sample 4*
- *More...*

I would love to contribute blogs, e-newsletter content, etc. Can we schedule a call to discuss how this opportunity can be mutually beneficial?

Thanks!
Rob Parker
(Signature)

The goal of this pitch is to get the call! So aim to get them on the phone ASAP!

Sharing the Love

I know it is easy to get caught up in getting exposure for your blog, but remember to take time commenting and engaging with other blogs also. Don't do it aimlessly though! Comment with the goal of gaining the attention of centers of influence, building relationships, building likeability, generating awareness, and promoting reciprocity. My suggestion is to spend time strategically commenting once a week for 15 to 20 minutes.

- Re-tweet other people's content
- @mention people on Twitter with their content
- Comment with an intelligent question. Foster a discussion.
- "Share" other people's Facebook posts

When used correctly, your website and blog should be the nucleus of your online presence.

CHAPTER 6

TWITTER: THE COCKTAIL PARTY

"Any idea, plan or purpose may be placed in the mind through repetition of thought." —Napoleon Hill

April 25th to April 28th, 2011 marked the largest single-system tornado outbreak ever recorded. Within the course of 72 hours, over 300 tornadoes ripped through over 20 states—a natural catastrophe that cost 324 lives and millions of dollars of devastating damage. Given the absolute destruction of the storms, local media stations and news reporters worked tirelessly to provide timely, rich coverage of the events.

In terms of top-notch coverage, Western Alabama's Tuscaloosa News, stood out from the crowd. And it wasn't because they offered rich updates via print and online. They used Twitter to report the latest on-the-ground details about the tornado, its damages, and the rescue and cleanup efforts. Some of their tweets are shown in the following graphic.

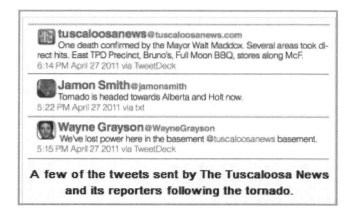

tuscaloosanews @tuscaloosanews.com
One death confirmed by the Mayor Walt Maddox. Several areas took direct hits. East TPD Precinct, Bruno's, Full Moon BBQ, stores along McF.
6:14 PM April 27 2011 via TweetDeck

Jamon Smith @jamonsmith
Tornado is headed towards Alberta and Holt now.
5:22 PM April 27 2011 via txt

Wayne Grayson @WayneGrayson
We've lost power here in the basement @tuscaloosanews basement.
5:15 PM April 27 2011 via TweetDeck

A few of the tweets sent by The Tuscaloosa News and its reporters following the tornado.

Because phone lines were jammed, "the first indications anybody was getting of how widespread this devastation was, was through [our reporters'] tweets," said City Editor Katherine Lee. Tuscaloosa's news coverage on Twitter had so much impact and was so relevant for the communities, that the station was later awarded with the Pulitzer Prize for breaking news.

This is only one of thousands of stories where Twitter has enhanced human communication. On the platform, people have discovered kidney donors, raised funds for important causes, and improved their business.

Take for instance the Dell Outlet. The company initially started using Twitter to promote their brand and push information out and soon found out that people were actually *interested*. Over time, they started using Twitter to not only raise awareness of deals, but also to interact with customers. By offering posts exclusively on Twitter, tracking URL's to discover which posts users find most intriguing, and offering top-notch customer service—Dell Outlet has booked more than $3 million dollars in revenue which can be attributed to Twitter posts. Research by the company also shows that the overall awareness of the outlet has expanded too.

It's not only big corporations and news stations reaping the benefits of Twitter. Realtors and other small business professionals are using it to communicate with prospects and increase exposure. According to Jude Boudreaux, a Certified Financial Planner, "I've met people through Twitter I wouldn't have met otherwise. Ultimately I'll get into people's consciousness, and when they're looking for a planner, I'll be the one they think of." @HJudeBoudreaux

Piggybacking on that story, I recently heard a loose statistic that 90% of people aren't ready to buy when you're ready to sell—but they will be ready within two years. I'm not sure if this stat is empirically accurate, but from what I've experienced I'd say it is. So how are you going to stay in front of prospects? How are you going to continually build trust and position yourself as an expert in your field? I'd say Jude is on to something.

The Bird's the Word

Twitter is, in many ways, the nexus of the social media revolution. Simple in nature and forceful in impact, this platform has revitalized the way we, as a culture, communicate. It breaks down barriers of time, space, and media proprietorship to connect real people and real stories in real time. It is freedom of speech and equality at its finest. To merely say it has "made an impact" wouldn't be enough, for it has shaken the communicative foundations of people, businesses, and establishments all across the globe.

As of August 2012, Twitter had over 175,000 active users – more than the entire continent of Australia. It also produces over 400,000,000 tweets produced per day. Now, that's a lot of chatter!

The birth of this social empire took place in 2006, when a bright group of board members from the broadcasting company, Odeo, sat around having a daylong brainstorming pow-wow. Unlike most brainstorming sessions, this one resulted in the creation of a groundbreaking social platform. The original project code, twttr, was developed for individuals using an SMS service to communicate with a small group. Later, the clan changed the name from twttr to what we now know as Twitter.

Twitter, as defined by dictionary.com, means, "to utter a succession of small, tremulous sounds, as a bird, or to talk lightly and rapidly, especially of trivial matters; chatter." The Odeo group agreed that this word captured the essence of the "in-the-moment," abbreviated communication social network.

What is Twitter?

As you may have already gathered, Twitter is a real time information network that connects people to the latest stories, ideas, opinions, and news all across the world. The most important aspect of Twitter is that it's always in the present moment. Other platforms like Facebook and LinkedIn move at a slower pace—conversations and posts can linger for days, whereas on Twitter, tweets will sometimes only last for seconds. Users pump information 24 hours a day, 7 days a week because the platform is by its very nature "in the moment."

> *Twitter is my favorite social platform because it's fast. There is always time for a tweet between things even in the busiest of days. I've really connected to some amazing people on Twitter in fact, that's how I met Amy and made it down to SXSW this year. I use Twitter to learn as well. Why spend hours digging for something interesting to write about when I can find a few of my favorite folks on*

twitter, have a quick scan of their tweets and presto I've got an idea. Blogging twice a week means you need to have ideas all the time!
-Stephanie Holmes, @TheMoneyFinder

Why Twitter?

Now, why should financial professionals use Twitter? I get this question all the time. In fact, many financial advisors still cast off Twitter as "useless." I am here, armed with real stories, to say they're wrong. If used correctly and strategically, Twitter is a business gem. Here's why:

- **Your audience is on Twitter:** With over 175 million (and counting) active users, it isn't a question whether or not your audience, in some form or another, is on Twitter. By having a presence, you build credibility for your brand and open the doors for millions who may be interested in what you offer.

- **Access to the media:** This is huge. Accessing local news stations and publications can be a daunting endeavor—especially for busy financial professionals. With Twitter, you have *instant* access to people and publications that will earn you the exposure your brand needs to increase referrals and local brand recognition.

- **Stay up-to-date on trends:** On Twitter, you're given moment-by-moment updates on what's going on in your local community and industry. This is key for staying on the cutting-edge trends, news, and ideas.

- **Don't have to accept people:** On LinkedIn and Facebook, you have to request and approve people in order to connect. With Twitter, those barriers don't exist. You can follow whoever you want. Reciprocally, anybody can follow you. If you are concerned about privacy, let it go. Twitter doesn't contain heavily private or personal information about you. Simply put, your profile has your picture, a 140-character bio, and a background. Its simple nature makes privacy a non-issue.

- **Reach high net-worth individuals:** Because there are no connection barriers on Twitter, you can reach and connect with influencers and high-net worth people. According to recent research conducted by Scorpio Partnership, a consulting firm, and sponsored by Standard Chartered Private Bank and SEI Global Wealth Service, more than 40 percent of high-net-worth individuals younger than 50 viewed social media as an important channel for communicating with their banks. If nothing else, this is brilliant way to get your brand in front of them.

- **Keep yourself in front of prospects:** Jude, the Certified Financial Planner, is a great example of how advisors can use Twitter. He merely engages in conversation, and keeps on the lookout for people who *just might be looking for a financial planner.* Perhaps more importantly, he serves as an educational resource. Who doesn't have questions about finances and retirement?

- **Customer service and damage control:** Several months ago some 7.5 million people in the UK faced the alarming reality that they had a lack of access to their earnings. The breaking news story was that NatWest had technical "glitches" and ultimately could not transfer money or pay wages.

As a result of this "glitch," customers could not pay bills, get home from work, get milk for their babies, or as one customer claimed, "check out of a hotel in Venice, missing a flight home." I'm sure we can agree that this is every company's worst nightmare, but when catastrophic situations arise, how do you control the way you deal with the problem? 10 years ago, the frustration associated with this situation would have been two-fold, due to clogged phone lines and lack of communication. In this instance, NatWest used Twitter to address customer concerns and keep angry customers informed about what was going on. This is a perfect example of how you can use Twitter in crisis situations. Just imagine if NatWest didn't have a Twitter account—they would've been helpless while thousands of angry customers posted negative comments.

Getting Started

Now that you have a foundational understanding of what Twitter is, let's get the ball rolling. Once you decide to create a Twitter page, here are a few steps to follow:

Create a "Handle"
When you visit www.twitter.com, your first order of business is to create an account, or "handle." Think of this like your email address on Twitter. I recommend using your name or company name. If you find it taken, however, try to abbreviate it and re-work the spelling. Avoid using the underscore symbol if possible.

Next, you need to create a profile background. Twitter offers several background templates that you can choose from. I suggest creating a customized background that aligns with your brand image. As a financial advisor, you may also want to consider adding contact information and disclaimers in your background (if your social media policy requires it).

For your profile description, use a tagline and/or language that aligns with your brand. Remember, you only have 140 characters to create a compelling message—so use powerful, to-the-point language that is rich with keywords.

Who Should You Follow?

Once you have your handle set up, you will be prompted to follow people. Before you start, think about the goals you have in mind for the specific demographic you'd like to reach. Start by following people you know, and build your feed by following people that you want to know. It's important to be selective when looking at these people. I'm sure you've seen a lot of profile descriptions that say "will follow back," but these are not the individuals you should be looking to add to your social networks. The purpose of Twitter (and many other social networking sites) is to build a solid networking foundation of prospective clients, current clients, industry leaders and partnering businesses. Simply following someone to build your numbers will not only clog your network, but it will damper your social media marketing commitment by blurring the intent, investment and return strategy. Here are some additional ideas:

- Local media stations (great precursor for getting PR exposure)
- Local newspapers
- People you *want* to know
- Financial publications
- Other businesses similar to yours
- Local chambers of commerce
- Industry leaders
- Social media thought leaders
- Better Business Bureaus
- Athletes
- Regulatory organizations like FINRA and the SEC
- Authors
- Editors of publications

Once you're following users, categorize them into lists. This will save you a *ton* of time while engaging on Twitter. Some examples of lists you'd create are: industry leaders, financial publications, local media, prospects, etc. Just think: if you log on to Twitter with the goal of gaining exposure for a recent article you published--you can go straight to local media and financial publications lists to promote your content. Lists are key for helping you target the right people at the right time.

Twitter Lingo 101

Let's be frank, learning Twitter lingo can feel like learning a foreign language. The first time I used the platform, I felt like an outsider entering a room with a million conversations happening at once--and I had no clue what was going on. In fact, my first tweet was "it's 5 o'clock." Yikes. For those of you familiar with the platform, you probably know exactly what I'm talking about. With the barrage of jargon and symbols, it isn't any wonder why you might be skeptical and confused at first. In fact, I'd be surprised if you weren't! Let's break it down into smaller pieces:

- **Tweets:** What in the heck is a "Tweet?" Tweets are the hallmark of Twitter, and are basically small bursts of information. Each Tweet (a.k.a. post) can only be 140 characters long, which challenges users to offer concise and rich information. Think of content as the selling point of your social media strategy – it's what should be attracting and retaining your followers. Don't tweet about just anything, take your time to research relevant newsfeeds that you know your followers would be interested in. With these powerful bite-sized messages, you can access a world of stories, news, ideas, conversations, photos, links, and videos directly at a glance, and all in one place. After giving Twitter a valid chance, I realized how much valuable information and intellect the world of Twitter had to offer. Over the years, I've discovered countless articles, perspectives, stories, and connections that have piqued my interest and expanded my awareness, both personal and professional.

- **A Re-Tweet or RT** is when someone shares a tweet by another person with their own followers. Several of my followers frequently re-tweet my content and I love them for it! It shows that they value my content enough to share it with *their* network. Let's be honest, getting re-tweeted feels like a million bucks! If you want to position yourself in front of big-wigs and/or influencers, re-tweet their content. I bet they'll notice! *Remember: If someone RT's your content, don't forget to thank them. It's proper etiquette.

- **@replies or @mentions** are when someone tweets you directly or about you. It's similar to "tagging" someone on Facebook and when you @mention someone it is public for anyone to see. By adding the @ symbol in front of a user's name it turns their name into a hyperlink and connects back to the person's profile when clicked on. Use this feature to capture someone's attention or link to another user's profile. For example: "Tune into @9News at 8am to see my interview live with @ryansheckron!" or "@WSJ Great article on Tax Laws. Check out my recent blog on the topic and reach out if you need a resource."

> **Financial Soc Media** @FinSocMedia   7h
> Great blog post by @VictorGaxiola ht.ly/devx0 #llsmc
> Collapse ← Reply 🗑 Delete ★ Favorite

- **Direct message:** Like most other platforms, you can send direct messages to people that show up in their private inbox. In order to direct message a user they need to be following you back. Direct messaging on Twitter is like the communication frontage road. It's much more effective than trying to squeak your way through people's jam-packed e-mail inboxes. Remember: only 140 characters!

- **URL shortener:** Because the character limit in Twitter is only 140 characters it is good to shorten URL's. Use http://bit.ly/or http://tiny.ly/ to shorten the link you want to tweet about so it fits under this 140 character limit. Many link shortening sites actually track the number of clicks each URL receives. This is great for learning what your audience is most receptive to.

- **"Favoriting"** is a great way of keeping a record of any tweets that you want to refer back to, whether that's someone recommending you, testimonials, or interesting news. You can find all your favorite'd tweets in one convenient place on your profile.

- **Hashtags (#):** The first hashtag I saw on Twitter was #lovecoffee. *Um, what?,* my mind uttered. I soon learned that #lovecoffee was not associated with any number or pound. The # symbol was created organically by Twitter users as a way to categorize conversations. #lovecoffee is a public conversation on Twitter for people who—you guessed it—love coffee! Here is an example of what that looks like:

Nick Jones @njay425
Coffee Nation was a great start to my morning #lovecoffee
Expand

Once you send the tweet, you'll notice that #lovecoffee becomes a link. When you click on the link, you can access all the conversations pertaining to this topic.

How Can Using Hashtags Benefit Your Business?

Using hashtags can lead to increased exposure, more followers, higher engagement and interaction levels, strategic connections and much more. Possibly one of the biggest advantages of utilizing hashtags is the ability to increase the reach of your voice. Engaging in online discussions not only extends your online reach, it also allows you to reach your social media marketing goals, such as increased leads, higher website traffic, and more. Instead of sorting and searching for the right hashtags (which I often find myself doing), I've compiled an alphabetical list you can use and refer back to:

#401k	#longtermcare
#advisors	#liquidity
#budget	#moneymanagement
#bonds	#money
#boomer	#mortgage
#babyboomer	#NASDAQ
#data	#NSE
#debt	(NationalStockExchange)
#economy	#overvalued
#equity	#personalfinance
#financial	#retirement
#financialadvice	#socialfa
#financialnews	#stocks
#FINRA	#taxes
#finsev	#underwriter
#GDP	#variableannuity
#homeowner	#warrenbuffet
#investing	#wealthmanagement
#linkedfa	

Other hashtag tricks:

- When you attend a conference or event, like the Securities Industry and Financial Markets Association (SIFMA), use the appropriate hash for the event in your tweet (#SIFMA).

- You can use hashtags for current events. For example, during the banking crisis taking place with NatWest, people were using #NatWest and #NatWestcrisis to contribute to the discussion.
- To check out local and global hashtag trends, visit Trendsmap or Whatthetrend.
- StockTwits organizes conversations around the $TICKER tag (i.e. $AAPL) into "streams," making it easy to find ideas and information. Search for stocks, explore trending tickers and follow links to the stream of a related stock or an individual user. Anyone can get started by exploring and following the conversation... StockTwits created the $ prefix for stocks (e.g. $MSFT). Follow @stocktwits and go to Stocktwits.com for Real-Time ideas and stock conversations.

Many financial professionals have yet to discover these hidden gems, so this definitely gives you a leg up.

Tweeting Your Way to Success

How Often Should I Tweet?
Posting tweets on Twitter is like tossing sticks into a roaring river. They are here now, and then gone in an instance. For this reason, you can and should post as much as you can.

What Should I Tweet?
The great and maybe somewhat hard thing about Twitter is the large amount of content you should be putting out daily. Twitter is like a radio station – different users are listening in at different times, which means in order to keep your followers happy you should be putting out quality content on a consistent basis. When it comes to posting, tweet a balanced mix of information and keep it simple by using the 10-4-1 "Social Sharing Rule." For every 15 tweets, do 10 tweets with links to

articles from third party sources, 4 tweets with company updates or blog posts, and 1 link to a company landing page.
Tweets that are in direct response to other users are not
counted in this ratio. In addition to your company blog posts,
third party articles, landing pages and replies to conversations
and re-tweets, other tweet suggestions include:

- **Like a Facebook page**: "@RichLoPresti, thanks for the
  follow. Check out our Facebook page too!bit.ly.1234.ax"

- **Promote your email newsletter**: "Curious about how to
  use Twitter? Check out our newsletter for tips on how
  #advisors can use #Twitter bit.ly.12345.ax"

- **Share a video**: "New video about how advisors can use
  Twitter hashtags. Bet you'll be surprised! bit.ly.12345.ax"

- **Share an e-book or white paper**: "New white paper
  containing latest stats on Long Term Care. Check it out!
  bit.ly.12345.ax"

- **Promote and conduct a webinar:** During the webinar
  include a unique hashtag so that users can share appropriate nuggets of information with their followers.

- **Tweet about upcoming events:** "Client appreciation
  event tomorrow night! Don't forget to RSVP bit.ly.12.as"

- **Tweet a photo:** "New renovations in the office! What do
  you think?"

- **Tweet a poll:** "What's your favorite downtown restaurant? Let us know bit.ly.12345.a"

- **Ask for volunteers**: Beta test a product or service.

> *Social Media Secret:*
> *Be cautious. Whatever you put out there in cyberspace will remain there for a very long time. Be judicious in what you post.*

Building a Following

Ever wonder how some companies amass so many followers? Well, it goes back to the basics of good ol' networking: create valuable content and participate in the conversation. Social media is a dialogue, so start by listening to what others have to say! Listening in Twitter equates to a large following. With millions of people on Twitter, you need to reach out to them first, and you need to do it every day. This is the perfect platform to connect with just the right people.

If you currently have a Twitter account I bet you've had people start to follow you and you wonder: *who the heck is this?* You click on their profile, check out their bio and maybe their website, and if they seem interesting you decide to follow them back. Chances are that they followed you because they think you may have an interest in their product or service. They got your attention by following you first and that's what *you* need to be doing in your local community.

Other Pointers:

Stay Focused

Have you ever visited a ghost town? Vacant buildings, weeds, broken windows, abandoned sheds. Not only are they creepy, but they're extremely unattractive. I'm willing to assume you've never sought to re-visit any ghost town you've ever been to, right? Idle Twitter pages are more unattractive than no Twitter page. They scream "I don't care." Is that the message you want to send to 175 million people? If you invested in a billboard, you wouldn't want it to be outdated or blank. Same rules apply here. Tis' better to have no Twitter than an abandoned Twitter.

Don't Rely on Automation

There are myriad of awesome automation and scheduling tools like HootSuite.com, libraries of pre-approved content, and RSS Feeds that will work wonders in saving you a lot of time. But remember that social media is meant to happen in "real-time." Don't rely 100% on automation. Your audience aren't automatons, therefore your posts shouldn't be robotic. There is no hurt in using some tools to take a load off your back, as long as there is a healthy combination of automated and manual interaction.

"I'm not a huge fan of scheduling tweets unless I want tweets to go out while I'm doing something like teaching a bootcamp. If this is the case I will schedule tweets out during the times of that day we are discussing certain things. Twitter is my favorite social network and it's the easiest to spend short bursts of time working with it. I often do extra tweets on days when I might have a doctors appointment and I'm in the waiting room tweeting away, not wasting a second."

-Stephanie Holmes, My Money Finder, @themoneyfinder

Listen to Your Audience

Twitter is a great way to learn about your audience. Observe and record what gets the most traction. These splices of information will not only optimize your Twitter presence, they will also enhance your overall marketing efforts!

"One of the biggest mistakes that I see is self promotion. Don't self promote 100% of the time. Twitter is about building relationships." -Brittney Castro, @BrittneyCastro

Promote Your Twitter Handle

Some people like apples. Some like oranges. Similarly, people prefer some social networks over others. That said, promote your Twitter handle across all your social media networks so your followers have the opportunity and option to follow you via their favorite platform.

Now that you are armed with all this knowledge, how are you going to use it? Learn how James Cox got started.

Spotlight on Success with Jamie Cox @jamescoxiii

James A. Cox, III, Harris Financial Group, has spent his entire career helping clients retire from some of America's most established companies, including Verizon, Philip Morris, Dominion, AEP, and Progress Energy. Jamie holds an MBA from Virginia Commonwealth University, and his strong educational background and experience in the industry provide the foundation for his insights into such topics as retirement planning, investment strategies, interest rate environments and other factors that impact the global marketplace. Jamie, his wife Melissa, and their two sons, Ian and Cade, live in Mechanicsville, Virginia.

Q. How did you first get involved in social media?

I got "kicked in the pool", so to speak. I had a friend that told me I have to use these social networks. The first network I signed up with was Facebook. I had no idea what it was about. In fact, I remember asking "what happens when you post?" After I was shown, I said "Oh. That's it? I thought it was something grander."

I think that this is how most advisors initially approach social media. But once they get started, they realize it's not as complicated as they thought.

Q. Which social network do you find yourself using the most?

When I first started using social media, Twitter was the platform I understood the best. In essence, you can follow anyone and anyone can follow you. It is a place where you speak in a microphone and anybody that wants to hear what you're saying can go on and find it.

What most people don't realize about Twitter is that it's also a search engine. If you want to utilize Twitter's maximum value, it's essential to use the search function. I subscribe to different feeds from different searches to hear conversations and gain insights about the clients I want.

In addition to using it as a search function, I also use it to communication with the media and generate PR for my brand. Doing this on Twitter has allowed for me to gain higher recognition.

Q. Can social media be used to generate leads?

In the past year, I've turned an estimated 30 social media leads into actual clients. In my experience, Twitter has been a really great point of entry where I'll cross paths and communicate with people. If they are interested, they often check out my other social platforms to make sure I am a credible, qualified advisor. From there, I often connect and communicate with them on other platforms. Nurturing these social relationships has proved to be really beneficial for me.

Q. Can you take me through all the varied elements of your social-media efforts?

I spend about 3-4 hours a day on Twitter. When I am on the phone with people, I often follow them on Twitter shortly thereafter. And even though I am on there all the time, I try to listen, listen, listen as much as I can. If there is something important for me to say, then I'll say it. On Twitter, words are everything. What you say can and will be used against you. It is for this reason that I always re-read what I write and go back to delete if I'm concerned about something I might have said in the past.

Q. What kind of mistakes do people make when it comes to social media?

I'd say the biggest mistake that advisors make is not doing it!

I also think it's important to have a filter. Many people don't realize the implications of what they post, and for that reason, it's so important to monitor your word choice and always look back at what you said.

Another mistake I see is inconsistent personalities. It is very important that your personality on social media matches your real personality. I am not a funny guy in person, so I am not going to act like I'm funny on my social platforms. Don't be something you're not, because people will recognize it right away.

Q. Any other pointers about Twitter?

Direct messaging is a highly functional Twitter feature that makes it easy to stay out of the public sphere when communicating with people. If you need any element of privacy, this is a great tool.

I also suggest advertising on Twitter. In my experience, Twitter has a far greater click through rate than Facebook and it's very under-utilized. If people are actively looking for something, they can search for it and find it right down the middle of their screen. I've had great success with advertising on Twitter.

CHAPTER 7

LINKEDIN:
THE GOLF COURSE

---

*"Innovation distinguishes between
a leader and a follower."* —*Steve Jobs*

Imagine you're at a business after-hours event. At this event, hundreds of professionals from various industries are mingling, making connections, and passing out business cards. You know this is a golden opportunity to connect and build your network, but how do you filter through the fray of people to find strategic, mutually beneficial connections and leads?

LinkedIn is the virtual version of that situation. You can mingle amongst others in your industry, join specific groups and conversations and build beneficial relationships with people you would like to connect with, all from the comfort of your office chair. With LinkedIn profiles filled with job histories, educational backgrounds, and even resumes, your ability to network with relevant associates, clients, and leads is almost endless. All you have to do is log on.

Social Media Secret:
According to a 2011 study by Advisors Trusted Advisor (ATA)/Advisor One, LinkedIn is becoming one of the top marketing tactics that advisors are starting to add to their marketing arsenal. ATA Principal Mike Slemmer explains in a press release that, "Comparing this data to ATA's 2009 survey on business building, LinkedIn use has more than doubled and -- more significantly -- those responding that their firm disallows social media use has been halved, to 33% from 65%...moreover, the comments reflected a wide range of uses for social media that we didn't see in the 2009 results."

What is LinkedIn?

So what exactly is LinkedIn? Some like to refer to it as the "golf course" of social media—and for a good reason. LinkedIn is a business-oriented social networking site connecting millions of people worldwide. And it's growing. Fast. In 2012, the platform reports more than 161 million registered users in more than 200 countries and territories. Statistics also show that 2 people sign up for a LinkedIn account **every second** and an incredible 5.3 billion searches are expected on LinkedIn in 2012.

LinkedIn differentiates from other social networks because of its high degree of professionalism and business-networking focused culture. You won't see posts of your friend's vacation photos or amusing cartoons on LinkedIn. You will, however, see millions of conversations pertaining to your local network and industry. People are using LinkedIn in many ways. The most notable reasons are:

- To prospect and generate leads
- To discover valuable connections
- To network with others in your industry

- To increase brand exposure and to position your business as a leader
- To establish credibility as a business and/or individual
- To seek employees and/or employment
- To gain insights from discussions with experts in group

How are Advisors Using LinkedIn?

Financial advisors are one of the top industries on LinkedIn. According to 2012 LinkedIn statistics, 12.4% of users on LinkedIn are financial professionals. Furthermore, LinkedIn polled 463 financial advisors in the United States to gain insight of how they're using the platform— respondents included 139 advisors from wirehouses, 209 from broker-dealers, and 115 RIAs. Check out some of these stats!

- 71% of advisors claimed they use social networks to do business. Among those advisors, LinkedIn has an overwhelming lead over other networks.
- 91% of advisors on social media use LinkedIn, whereas no other network is used for business by even one-third of advisors. This is reflected in the large population of advisors on LinkedIn.
- More than 180,000 U.S. financial advisors use the network. They also use it more frequently than any other platform.
- 53% of advisors on LinkedIn use the network at least once a week, and 74% use it at least once a month.

Advisors are Seeing Results

Yeah, yeah, yeah, so advisors are on LinkedIn, but is it making a difference? The answer is yes. Many advisors using social media are seeing real business results from it, in terms of both clients and assets. The 2012 survey also showed that:

- More than 60% of them have used LinkedIn to gain new clients.

- Of that group, 32% used LinkedIn to bring in $1 million or more in assets under management.

The successful advisors are also using LinkedIn across many facets of their business lifecycle, especially during the early phases:

- Improving the effectiveness of referral network: 75%
- Cultivating client prospects: 72%
- Building my brand identity: 61%
- Enhancing current client relationships: 55%

Increasing numbers of advisors are also using LinkedIn to expand their own professional knowledge and to share thought leadership with their connections.

Social Media and High Net Worth Investors
In a separate survey, LinkedIn published the results of more than 600 high net worth (HNW) investors in the United States and Canada. That survey offered clear findings of how financial advisors address the HNW market via social media.

One key finding is that **more than 5 million HNW investors are actively using social media to help them make financial decisions.** Of that group, 73% use LinkedIn, and they use it more than Facebook and Twitter. The survey also showed that investors tend to be more active in their investment habits, doing more research online and making more trades.

Here are some other pertinent findings:

- **Only half of the HNW investors active on LinkedIn have financial advisors,** whereas about 80% of HNW investors not active on social media already have advisors.

That could mean a huge prospecting opportunity for advisors using LinkedIn.

- Of investors who already have advisors and use social media, **more than half (52%) say that they would like to interact with their advisor using social media — yet only 4% of them actually do.** Again, this could mean a major opportunity for advisors to build rapport to retain existing clients and increase their assets under management.

- High Net Worth individuals, in conjunction with the broader population, are increasing their use of social media. There is a world of untapped opportunity, particularly on LinkedIn, for financial advisors to pioneer.

> *"Clearly the business opportunities lie with LinkedIn. You can learn so much about your prospects before you even meet them. I fully expect it to be a major source of our business in the coming years."*
>
> –Dan Cuprill
> @DanCuprill

Affluence
LinkedIn is unquestionably the most affluent of the major social media platforms. Again, these statistics speak to the value of LinkedIn for financial professionals.

- 39% of members are managers, directors, owners, chief officers, and vice presidents.
- According to a 2012 Consumer Electronics Report, 49% of LinkedIn users have household incomes over $100,000. The survey also suggests that users are more likely to own tablets and smartphones.

Getting Started: Setting Up and Optimizing Your Profile
With over 175 million professionals on LinkedIn, how are you going to make yourself a diamond in the rough? The proliferation of LinkedIn as a professional resource for individu-

als and businesses to connect and expand their social networks has created a need for some bare-bones advice on how to create and develop an optimized LinkedIn profile. There are myriad reasons to make your presence known on the LinkedIn network. If optimized and used efficiently, it can be used to bring in more money and job opportunities, network with peers, industry leaders, and other professionals, receive and provide professional recommendations, add a face to your business, and offer a valuable offshoot to your website.

Social Media Secret: Did you know that users with complete profiles are 40 times more likely to receive opportunities through LinkedIn?

Keywords

A keyword is a term that people use when trying to find you. On LinkedIn, it's essential that you optimize your profile around keywords you want to get found by. For example, if you're a retirement planner, you'd want to optimize your profile so that when people search for "retirement," your profile is first – or at least on the first page. To do this, you need to make sure key terms recur multiple times in your current job titles, past job titles, personal summary, and company summary. Here is what you can do to achieve the best results:

- Use long tail keywords: For example, instead of using "financial advisor" as your primary keyword, use something more narrow and specific like "financial and retirement advisor."
- Use keywords generously throughout your profile: Once you have a list of keywords that are the most pertinent to you and your business, use them recurrently throughout your profile in your current job titles, past job titles, personal summaries, and company summaries.

Headlines

The headline of your LinkedIn page is really important! It is the first impression, and we all know that first impressions create lasting impressions. Here are a few strategies for creating good headlines:

- Use three titles per headline and separate them with |. This makes your headline more comprehensive.
- Avoid filler words. For example, use "&" instead of writing out "and." It saves space.
- Use keywords frequently, include the location, and make the headlines encompassing of the services you offer.

Here is an example of a powerful LinkedIn headline:

Personal Summary
- Speak of yourself in the 3rd person ("He" has been a financial advisor for two decades).

- Include a brief intro about yourself, how you got into the industry, your education/designations, and a little information about your personal interests.
- Use strong language. For example, don't just say "Bob helps people plan for retirement," say "Bob is passionate about preparing clients for a comfortable retirement."

Sample:

As co-founder and managing partner at Smith Financial, Bob Smith specializes in assisting clients with investment planning, estate planning, and health care concerns. With over two decades of experience as a CERTIFIED FINANCIAL PLANNER™ and over 20 years of investment experience, he provides clients financial advice and investment strategies to help them meet their goals and dreams.

Bob earned his B.S. in business administration in 1985 from The University of Colorado at Boulder, and in 1986 was registered as a securities representative. Along with his CFP designation, Bob currently holds Series 7, 24, 63 and 66 Registrations along with multiple Life and Health Insurance Licenses.

In 1992, after experiencing the ineffectiveness of numerous regional brokerage firms that merely offered static "investment products" and simply wanted to reach "sales quotas," Bob adopted a service-based financial assistance model based on the needs and best interests of the clients. And so, Smith Financial was born. The team at Smith consists of independent financial advisors specializing in financial planning for individuals and small businesses.

Company Bio

After your personal summary, include a short company summary. If you have a company summary or mission statement on your website that you feel is strong, use it. Here are some basic suggestions for a standout company summary.

- Use keywords over and over.
- Use powerful verbs like passionate, committed, devoted, adamant...
- Illustrate your company values and create images of prosperity and success.
- Include all of the specialties/services of your business.
- Keep it relatively short. 100-150 words is a good length.

Sample:

Balanced Wealth Management is passionate and committed to building long-lasting, mutually satisfying relationships rooted in financial growth and success. With over 20 years of experience, we offer clients the honest, straightforward investment advice needed for success. Through financial education and coaching, clients achieve the knowledge and tools to pursue their loftiest financial goals via structured mutual funds, efficient, tax-favored cash value life insurance strategies, 401(k)'s, IRA's, guaranteed lifetime income annuities, and no cost mortgage purchase and refinance solutions. Achieve financial balance and prosperity at Balanced Wealth Management.

Websites

LinkedIn gives you the ability to add up to three websites to your profile. Take advantage of this. Utilize all three options with your website, your blog site, your Facebook link, links to external associations you are part of or other relevant options. Not only do these provide an easy outlet for your connections to view your information, but it also can aid in your SEO strategy. Whenever you include links to external sites, use calls to action. For example, instead of saying "Smith Financial Website," say "Check out Smith Financial!"

Building Your Network

There are many ways to approach connecting on LinkedIn. While we strongly suggest you connect with anyone and everyone, there are multiple approaches you can take. Social Media Sonar has 4 encompassing connection strategies:

- **The Lion:** Lions are completely open connectors. They seek to increase their connections through actively sending out and accepting connection invitations. While I'm sure there are a few who take pride in touting the specific number, the majority believe that large networks lead to more opportunity.

- **The Turtle:** Turtles are the opposite of lions. Turtles primarily connect with those they know well. They see value in having a tight network made up of individuals they completely trust. Their networks tend to be highly selective and can be counted on to pass on introductions, much like a private networking group.

- **The Hound Dog:** A Hound Dog is someone who uses LinkedIn to connect to those they know and those they would like to know. They also accept invitations from those that would be beneficial to be connected to.

- **The Alley Cat:** Alley cats only send invitations to people they know or people they have a specific reason for connecting to, but they accept invitations from just about anyone. They believe there is value in knowing your connections, but there are also unexpected opportunities that develop from establishing new connections— known and unknown.

There is value in utilizing all of these strategies and we suggest you use your best judgment. Regardless, you need to be connecting.

Who to Connect With?
Who should you connect with on LinkedIn?

- People in your industry
- Marketing experts
- Prospects
- Present and past colleagues
- People you meet at conferences
- Professional friends

Targeted Searches
LinkedIn gives you the ability to target your searches to a very specific demographic that can be incredibly valuable in terms of connecting and sending messages. Are you hosting a wine tasting event in Atlanta for prospective clients? LinkedIn allows you to search for people in the Atlanta area, in the desired age and financial demographic, with a mention of wine in their profile. You can't get more targeted than that!

Personalization
Have you ever talked to an automated voice recorder on the phone or received automated messages online? If you haven't, it's very frustrating. We are not automatons, we're humans with an innate desire to feel important and have genuine human connection. LinkedIn prompts you to send messages to connections on numerous occasions—i.e. requesting connections, accepting connection requests, or sending recommendation requests. Instead of using the generic, automated message LinkedIn provides you, create personalized message templates.

Integration

Often times your connections on LinkedIn will differ from your fans and followers on your other social media sites. It is important to use LinkedIn to build your audience on your other sites. You can easily send a message to your connections inviting them to check out your Facebook fan page or follow you on Twitter. We already discussed how you can target specific demographics with your connections, now that you have captured them, you can invite them to engage further through your other platforms as well.

Connect to Groups

Groups are gold mines in the LinkedIn world. Whether you're seeking to find valuable connections, increase brand exposure, or simply be aware of industry trends, groups will help you achieve all of these objectives. When connecting with groups, try to aim for 75% potential client and 25% industry connection to learn from your peers. Also seek out local and personal interest groups—such as St. Louis Business Exchange, Denver Ski Club, or Golf and Business Networking.

Think: What groups are my potential clients connected to? What interests do they have in common? What groups can I gain valuable business exposure? Where are the industry leaders at?

How else can you use groups?

- To post blogs, surveys, discussions, and articles—some groups have an upwards of 10,000 members. That's a ton of potential exposure for your brand.
- To start and engage in conversations about pertinent industry topics.
- To seek potential clients, leads, and/or business connections.
- To observe and learn from industry leaders.

Recommendations

IMPORTANT NOTE: As a Registered Representative or RIA skip over this next section as recommendations are considered endorsements and are prohibited by FINRA and the SEC. More info on this topic can be found later in the chapter on compliance.

On LinkedIn, you can amass an unlimited number of recommendations, which is powerful social proof of your credibility. In essence, you invite others to compose a concise recommendation to showcase your accreditations, accomplishments, and performances for the whole network to see. There's no greater testimonial for your capabilities than the words of someone else who's worked with you. A great way to get recommendations is by recommending someone else first. More often than not, they will return the favor. In fact, LinkedIn prompts them to do so when they choose to accept your recommendation.

You can also send a note to your connections asking for their recommendation. LinkedIn provides some nice basic copy but go ahead and personalize it for the best results. The more recommendations the better, so don't hesitate to ask.

LinkedIn Company Pages
Company Pages are one of the hallmark features of LinkedIn. They consist of a company profile and aggregated statistics about employees. The utilization of Company Pages can drive traffic, increase revenue, and get your brand seen by more prospective clients. It is not only a great way to track and monitor your past, present and future employees, but it is also an excellent addition to your social media marketing campaign.

Company Pages are the best forum to advertise your brand and its products or services on LinkedIn. It is the perfect opportunity in promotions because of its layout and scope within LinkedIn. You can add your Company Page to your current (or past) job title. You can also add links to your company page outside of LinkedIn. Driving traffic to your Company Page will in turn drive traffic to your company website, increasing your client traffic, as well as your revenue.

The Company Profile is a short overview of the company-what industry it is in, where it is located, what services it provides, and other pertinent information. Like your personal summary, use strong verbs and make sure it concisely encompasses your company.

The company directory offers a list of all employees at that company who are members of LinkedIn. Connect with them. Send them a message. Let them know that you work with some of their co-workers. Or, better yet, ask your clients (who are hopefully a connection already) to send you an introduction through LinkedIn. This is an incredibly powerful benefit of company pages that will really help with referrals and reaching targeted prospects.

• **Prospecting with Company Pages:** With company pages, you can make adjustments so you are notified anytime someone is hired, promoted, or leaves a company. This is an excellent opportunity to contact these individuals about 401(k) rollover or pension options! You can also adjust to be notified with network updates and email digest.

When following companies, you will also receive information about the company, including how many followers they have, where employees call home, the most common skills of employees, and the most recommended employees at the company. This can also be a great prospecting tool.

- **Related companies** find trends in the work history of users and identifying connections between companies. You can see where employees have worked before, where they went after they left, and which other companies they are related to. For example, the first LinkedIn user listed is Stuart, and he came from O'Charley's, and was the corporate director of beverage. This is a great asset to have to keep track of current and past employees.

- **Key statistics** are produced from the aggregated non-personally identifiable data of LinkedIn users who are currently employed by the company. Such statistics include, but are not limited to—top schools the company hires from, most popular location the company hires from or location where its employees reside, most viewed profiles, and much more. Most viewed profiles, or popular profiles are LinkedIn users who are highlighted because they may be actively in the news, referenced in blogs, participating in industry groups, and frequently the result of searches and other activities within the LinkedIn network. This is great information if you are the owner or managing partner and wish to see which employees in your company are active within your company's network.

Company Pages will drive traffic to your business, increase revenue and get your brand out in front of more possible clients. Not only will it help your business track its employees and monitor its aggregate growth and changes, but it will act as an excellent addition to your marketing campaign.

Upgrading to Pro

LinkedIn also offers a Pro option for their profiles. Despite all the abilities and capabilities of the basic accounts, Pro accounts offer even more networking services. One of the most desirable of these is the ability to send a limited amount of what are called "InMail" messages. LinkedIn limits who you can contact based on the degree of connection you share with them, but InMail allows you to message people even if you have no prior connection to their profile. This InMail is the equivalent of making a cold-call in sales, but widens your connection and communication ability. Pro accounts also offer opportunities to segment your connections into folders based on certain characteristics and allows you to target specific groups for specific communications. The downside? These perks come with a cost, anywhere from $40-$100 a month. With all that LinkedIn basic accounts have to offer, most people are happy to keep their free profiles and build their network from there.

CHAPTER 8

YOUTUBE:
THE HOLLYWOOD

---

*"If you aren't getting picked up by the
radio and news stations - create your own."*
-Mark Matson

Before the birth of the internet and social media, there was an illusive barrier between those on television and radio, and those who were not. In fact, the 'barrier' was so profound that it elevated those on television and radio to a certain stardom. Unless you had access to the media, it was rare to establish your own television or radio station. It was even more unlikely that you'd generate a robust and committed following. You listened. You watched. And the window to inch your way into the spotlight was ever so slight.

With the development of social media, however, there is no longer a barrier between the bleachers and the playing field. With a mere video recorder, camera, or even cell phone, you can upload videos to your very own YouTube channel in a matter of seconds. This simple ability has transformed the way that we, as a global community, communicate. It's quite remarkable--for it has increased democratization and established a unique space for people, businesses, and organizations to spread their message and get their voices heard.

For those that are unfamiliar, YouTube is a platform for original content creators and people all across the globe to connect, inform, and inspire others via short videos. There are millions of people that watch millions of videos every day on YouTube. In fact, more content is uploaded to YouTube in a 60 day period than the three major U.S. television networks created in 60 years. This means that 800 million people across the globe have access to your voice. Eight. Hundred. Million. And the numbers are only increasing. Within the next decade, I anticipate YouTube to eclipse other major media stations in terms of viewership.

I'm sure you're wondering—*So what? As a Financial Professional, how can I use this platform for my business?* What type of videos would I upload? How can I stay compliant? By the end of this chapter, I can assure you'll have an abundance of valuable information when it comes to weaving YouTube into your marketing strategy.

How Advisors are Using YouTube

Millions of businesses are using YouTube—but how are financial professionals, as a niche, using the platform? Matson Money, Inc. is one of the few financial firms that have fully delved into YouTube--and the company has seen huge results. With several hundred subscribers and well over 60,000 views, Matson Money's weekly series, Matson Money Live, has set the stage for how to achieve success on Youtube. And they began the same way you will. They created a plan and dove in.

The question is: how can *your firm* gain exposure and achieve the same results with YouTube? First and foremost, it's essential to discuss the overall purpose of YouTube. For many financial professionals, this is to establish credibility and increase exposure. Similar to your blog, you want to position yourself as the expert in your videos. By producing interesting, useful, and timely content, you send the message that "I know what I'm talking about." This is key to retaining clients and attracting leads and potential clients.

From a topical standpoint, Matson creates videos that address a plethora of financial topics. Some examples are: "The Benefits of International Investing," "How to Build an Inefficient Portfolio," and "Real People, Real Problems." The College Funding Connection also has videos that engage their target audience while establishing credibility— "Why so Many Middle Class Parents Pay so Little for Children's College Education?" (Part 1 of 7) and "Why High School Financial Aid Nights can be Hazardous to your Wealth!" (Part 2 of 7).

Similar to the other social platforms, the key here is putting yourself in the shoes of your consumer. If you were a potential client, what would you want to watch?

Stop Paying to Rent an Audience

By creating powerful content, you build a following--'fans' so to speak. Just think, if you were to run a news or radio ad, you would essentially be "renting" their audience for a brief period of time. But if you have a well-rounded, established YouTube channel, you can build your OWN audience. An audience that is loyal and interested in you. The larger and more engaged the audience, the more power and influence you'll have.

Strategies for Going Viral

Did you know that Google owns YouTube? That means that by signing up for YouTube, you are building a friendship with the largest search engine in the world. Google loves to give preferential search engine treatment for YouTube videos. Therefore, by creating a YouTube account you're already well on your way to boosting your search engine rankings. But it doesn't end there. What are some other strategies for increasing viewership?

Length
The optimal length for a video is a gray area. You have a maximum of 15 minutes for your video. But before you max out the length, make sure you're effectively getting your message across while engaging the audience. If you use the entire 15 minutes, the video better be extremely engaging and entertaining. Psychologists have noted that the average sustained attention span of an adult is 20 minutes. But for online videos, it seems to be about 60 seconds before people lose interest. To hover on the safe side, make your video 60-90 seconds. Research indicates that viewers have a short attention span and, more often than not, will quit watching your video if it's longer than that.

Creating a Hook Title
Do a little keyword searching on Google AdWords to see which terms and phrases get searched the most, and have the least competition. Remember to make it short and emotionally triggering.

Entertaining
The most highly viewed videos on YouTube are entertaining and have some degree of shock effect. This doesn't mean

your video has to contain outlandish content, but it helps to integrate humor, quirkiness, honesty, and perhaps a dash of controversy. Similar to your blog, speak to your audience. What are the pressing issues in their lives? What do they want to hear and learn about? How can you address them in a unique, engaging manner?

Interviews and Stories

To add an extra flare to your video library, aim to integrate relevant interviews and stories. Perhaps you know somebody who can share interesting experiences or insights about retirement or 401(k) planning. Or maybe you know of an individual that paid off his/her credit card debt who can offer advice to others. Be creative. Your videos don't have to be strictly informative, they can be awe-inspiring too.

How-To's

There will always be a demand for "how-to" and Q&A videos. What are some of the frequently asked questions that you receive as a financial advisor? What are topics that people struggle with or are unsure of? At FSM, We love to create videos and blogs that address real concerns we have with clients and also client testimonials. You should do the same.

Don't Make It an Ad

Steer clear of explicit self-promotion. People don't want a commercial, they want rich, engaging content. There are billions of videos on YouTube–do you think people are going to waste their time watching a self-promoting piece? Instead, include brief calls to action, such as "download our free compliance guide to learn more" or "visit our blog to learn more about budgeting."

> *"One of the biggest mistakes people make on social media is too much self-promotion. My rule is to promote 3-4 other people before you promote yourself."*
> *–Jeff Rose, Good Financial Cents, @jjeffrose*

Four Key Elements

According to Dr. Brent Coker, a marketing professor at the University of Melbourne, the four key elements required for a video to go viral are:

- Congruency: The themes of a video must be congruent with people's pre-existing knowledge of the brand it is advertising.
- Emotive strength: Creating strong emotions is essential if you want to ensure you are giving your video the best chance of becoming viral and the more extreme the emotions, the better.
- Network involvement: Videos must be relevant to a large network of people and the larger the better, some examples of large networks are college students or office workers.
- "Paired meme synergy:" These memes can be elements such as humor or unexpectedness. When you create your videos, aim to deviate from the norm and engage your audience in unique ways.

Here are 16 meme strategies he dubbed for viral success:

BVMP MEME ELEMENTS (UNPAIRED)	
Cutsie Wootsie	Vigilante Justice
Impromptu	Eyes Surprise
Disruption Destruction	Baby Love
Performance	Nostalgic Bubblegum
Anticipation	Voyeur
Simulation trigger	Rose Glasses
Skill Bill	Comedy Side Split

© Brent Coker 2011

SEO and Weaving Videos on Other Platforms

YouTube is an incredibly utilitarian platform. Once you've established a personalized channel and built a video library, you can feature your videos anywhere. In fact, I recommend that you embed and weave your videos into all of your social platforms, including your website, to maximize marketing results. Post them to your Facebook, LinkedIn, and Twitter, embed it in your blog, submit it to StumbleUpon, create a video board on Pinterest, and send it in your e-newsletter and mailing list. Blast the video everywhere! In addition to posting the video to your social networks, Social Media Today offers some additional advice on video SEO:

- **Title:** Make sure your targeted keywords are in the first few words of your title. Another trick is to add a colon after your initial keywords and rephrase your title for maximum effect. For example, your video on saving money for college might be called "College Savings Plans: The 529 Plan and Your Child."

- **Description:** Two things to keep in mind here: 1) start your description with a full URL, and 2) don't be stingy with your description—more is… well, more. Be as descriptive and keyword-rich as possible. This will help you get found more easily by people searching YouTube for your type of content. You can also include more URL's throughout your content.

- **Tags:** Be sure to include any and all related keywords in the tags field.

Types of Videos

So you have a YouTube channel, now what? What type of video content should you create? Here are some ideas:

- **Welcome videos:** If you create a short welcome video, the link can be shared in newsletters, social media and via email. Your current clients can simply share a link with a friend or family member who is looking for a new advisor. A short video allows you to connect with people in a way that is virtually impossible to do on paper. It allows you to make an impact and make an impression. When a new client walks into your office, they will feel like they already have a relationship with you. Include a brief story about your background, hobbies, favorite sports team, family or business and you'll be surprised how many people will ask you about it. -Kristi Piehl | Owner, Media Minefield | media-minefield.com

- **Educational:** When it comes to the financial industry, there is so much to learn. There is also a lot of misinformation out there. Why not create educational videos that address topics that are important to your audience? As long as you don't offer specific, one-size-fits-all financial advice, this can be an incredibly powerful resource for your prospects and clients.

- **Guest interviews:** Not sure what to say or do for your video? Why not invite a guest speaker to come and do a live interview? Brittney Castro, CFP® is a true pioneer of this strategy. On her YouTube channel, Financially Wise Women, she brings in a wide range of professionals to interview--from yogis to law professionals--to discuss their professional and financial lives. The question that ties all of the interviews together is, "what does it mean to you to be a financially wise woman?" This strategy has earned her over 13,000 views on her channel.

- **Financial news:** Broadcast pertinent and relevant financial news. We have several clients that like to do a weekly financial news recap to inform their audience about the most important financial discussions taking place and how it will affect them.

- **Themed shows:** Piggy backing on the financial news idea, you can also develop themed shows where you talk about financial related topics. Perhaps you have guest speakers or interviews. The goal here is to keep your audience interested and engaged.

- **Video responses:** This is very popular in the YouTube world. Is there a television show, blog, article, current event, debate, or story that you want to comment on? YouTube is the perfect place to do it. Create a short video of yourself responding to an important issue. If you season it with slight controversy, it is likely to pique the interest of your audience.

- **Human interest:** Your videos don't just have to be financial related. You can create videos about a whole plethora of topics--travel, golf, culinary, wine and spirits, the Olympics, you name it. As long as it aligns with your audience's interests, it's okay to weave in some human interest bits. Bryan Weiss of Marion Financial Partners created a YouTube video called "You Won't Believe what I saw on the Golf Course..." In this video, he talks about an abnormal situation he ran into on the golf course and then related it back to investing. This is a creative way to pique interest and offer insight.

- **Video for landing pages:** When it comes to website landing pages, the purpose is to capture your visitor's attention and incentivize them to want to learn more by entering their contact information, making a purchase, or simply driving them to a different part of your website. With video being the hot commodity in marketing, it's no surprise that more and more organizations are choosing to optimize their landing pages with video. Moreover, adding video to your landing pages will improve opt-ins and click-throughs by up to 70%.

When you are creating your landing page it's important to experiment with your registration fields and video topics. Typically, the more information required to complete a registration form will lead to a decrease in conversions. This is also typical when video length increases. The trick? Keep everything short, simple and to the point! Don't stray from the purpose of the video and the landing page – to convert visitors to potential leads.

Tips for Production

If you've ever written, created, recorded and edited a video, you know how difficult and tedious it can actually be. First off, writing a compelling and engaging script that will entice your audience to continue watching is a complex and creative task. Fortunately, there are several things you can keep in mind to ease the stress of producing a video.

- Keep it short: you have approximately seven to fifteen seconds to explain to your listener what your video is about. Think about it like the topic sentence of an article or story.
- Explain the benefits of opting in and how it will be of value to them.
- Have a clear call to action: tell them what to do!
- Be yourself! The last thing a listener wants to hear is some monotonous voice trying to sell them something. Be charismatic and engaging.
- Give thanks: always end your video by giving the listener an appreciation of their time and attention.

When it comes to recording the video, it's important to realize that the imagery of your video is just as important as the message. The background, your clothing and even your hair need to match your message.

- Don't make the background distracting. Your background should match your message, so if you're trying to promote your business, don't record your video in your bedroom or a random setting.
- Dress professionally.

- Speak clearly and look directly into the camera – it should feel like the person on the camera is talking directly to the listener.

Editing your video is key to enhancing and making your video even more creative.

- Add background music or additional animations that match your message.
- Add your logo and company information at the beginning and the end of your video.

The final elements of optimizing your usage of the video is uploading your video to YouTube, embedding it on your landing page, site or profiles and adding content.

- Keep your most important content above the fold. Your conversation rates will increase if visitors don't have to scroll down to complete your form.
- Limit your visitors' options: exclude additional links or other items that will distract visitors from the purpose of the video.
- Appeal to skimmers: many of your visitors may be individuals not searching out a specific product or service. It's for this reason that you need to make use of headers, sub-headers, bold text, bullets, white space, and graphics such as arrows or buttons to draw a reader's eye towards your call to action.

It is important to remember that you don't have to have a cast and crew on a Hollywood stage and a big production company to make a successful video. The usage of a webcam and microphone will serve just as well. People will watch your videos because you are an expert in your field with information relevant to them. A simple production effort will do just the trick.

If you want to stay on the cutting edge of online marketing, it is essential to build a branded YouTube account and use it as much as possible. With the rapid growth of videos, it would not be surprising if they completely replaced written content within the next few years. Now is the time to jump on the bandwagon.

Spotlight on Success by Michelle Matson, Matson Money, Inc.

Matson Money, Inc first became aware of social media through a marketing conference in early 2008. Until that point, networks like Facebook and YouTube seemed more like entertainment for teenagers than a tool we would use to help our investment business. When we started to see more and more marketers using social networks to spread their message, we decided to see what we could do with it too.

Our first video was shot and posted in late summer of 2008–it had fewer than fifty views. In comparison to the many viral videos on the internet that might seem like a failure, but we realized that we could build on that number and actively engage our existing advisors and clients to participate and communicate with us in a new way. We didn't need a video to go viral in order to reach the audience that we wanted to reach.

We realized that we needed to master the process of quickly shooting video, editing, uploading, posting and communicating about each video. For the subsequent six months, we focused on building the infrastructure to support regular videos and email communications to promote them. We had to purchase cameras, build blog sites that would become the hub for the videos, write compliance policies, and create a system and process for communicating with each new post.

Four years later, we post three to five new videos each week, with over 50,000 views on videos and nearly two million minutes of viewing time of our videos and live web broadcasts.

Through the use of YouTube we have built stronger relationships with financial professionals and investors alike. We have communicated important messages during one of the most difficult market cycles in recent memory. Social media and video, in particular, allows us to get the exact message across that we need to communicate in an extremely timely manner.

We jumped into the social media realm with both feet and know it can be overwhelming to understand and implement more than one type of social network at a time. The best advice we can give is to take one social network and learn how it works, what is the right content for that network and how you want to use your voice, then move on to the next one. The more you use these networks and get familiar with them, the more they will help you leverage the time it takes to communicate with your audience. They are an amazing tool for leveraging your time and solidifying relationships with clients.

Michelle Matson
@michellematson

CHAPTER 9

COMPLIANCE:
WHAT YOU NEED
TO KNOW

"The door to safety swings on the hinges of common sense." -Unknown

As you have seen so far - social media is a combination of broadcast, engagement, listening outpost and conversation place (i.e. water cooler). Knowing this also informs how we approach the rules that govern our use of social platforms and our expanding connections.

While there has been much debate over exactly what the rules are - we can distill it down to what FINRA and the SEC have told us:

- A social media policy is a must as step one
- Your policy will then define your written supervisory procedures

- Social media archiving is an essential ingredient – having a central dashboard that you control – where you perform record retention and surveillance
- Understanding and complying with the differences in static and interactive content

These fundamentals will get you started as well as ensure you comply with the core areas of regulatory concern.

To provide a thorough understanding of compliance, we enlisted some help! The following chapter was co-written with Blare Warrene and the team at Arkovi, a leading social media archiving provider.

Getting Started

Compliance Fundamentals

1. A books and records maintenance requirement for communications
2. A prohibition against the use of testimonials
3. A policy for the security and protection of customer information
4. A written supervisory policies requirement
5. A Code of Ethics

Social media is directly impacted through each of these regulatory obligations. Thus any misuse or inappropriate content or comments on the investment advisor's or the investment advisor representative's social media site(s) could easily violate SEC, state and/or firm policy.

Mitigating risk around the use of social media involves three clear steps:

1. Identify your strategy for incorporating social media into communications
2. Establish and define your guidelines and policies
3. Deploy the tools to use, archive, monitor and report on social media

Doing so reduces opportunities for your firm to become subject to regulatory sanctions, civil litigation and/or negative publicity.

The initial response to the use of social media has been for investment advisors to prohibit or severely restrict the usage to perhaps a LinkedIn profile.

With the exploding popularity of social media as a communications tool, and the statistics showing the rapid growth in social media usage by financial professionals, expectations of compliance with a full prohibition as a firm policy is most likely unrealistic.

The better approach is to be proactive. Accept the reality that it is being actively used in practice and develop reasonable policies and procedures to address its usage. A secondary benefit of this strategy is that the you can now incorporate social media into a marketing strategy without being in conflict with your own social media policy.

One caveat in developing a social media policy is the need for the developer to understand and accept the relative immaturity of the medium. While e-mail as a medium is relatively built out and fairly easy to monitor and archive on a proprietary level, social media has not yet reached this level of maturity. Social media comes to us in a wide variety of products and feature sets that are constantly adapting as they undergo further development.

While review and archival solutions are being developed as soon as the primary social media developers release access to content and features they have developed, the reality is that a totally complete solution will never be possible as long as new social media features are continuing to be developed. The best that one can hope to accomplish is pre-review of some content, mediation and archival capabilities. With this reality in mind, developers of social media policies will need to acknowledge the inherent limitation and tailor their policies around what is possible to control.

In certain instance these limitations will need to be addressed with limited feature prohibitions but overall a viable and more importantly manageable social media policy is possible. In the rubric of the broker dealer world one should establish a policy that is reasonably designed to achieve compliance with applicable SEC investment advisory rules.

A Social Media Policy and Brand Protection
By embracing social media, you are opening your business up to interacting and communicating online using a variety of social networks. It is a best practice to map out ethics and governance rules for your team members. Interacting with customers online is different than talking to them face to face, which is exactly why a policy is necessary. A business is always responsible for brand protection – a social media policy allows everyone using social media to acquaint themselves with the do's and don'ts of online interaction, as well as what audience they should be communicating with. Here are three basic guidelines to keep in mind when communicating online and upholding your brand integrity:

1. Be aware of who is viewing your information and what is being shared.
   o Don't panic if you receive a negative comment – these interactions give you the chance to display your great customer service skills.

o   If it is a credible issue, respond in a timely matter, listen to your customer, and take the necessary actions to improve.
2.   Provide your followers with positive and credible information.
o   Share information that establishes yourself as an influencer and reliable source in the financial services industry.
o   Credible information leads to trust and speaks volumes about your brand online.
3.   Be open to opinions.
o   Once again, social media is all about interaction, so keep an open mind and listen to others online – you'll build more customer relationships this way.

What to Address in a Social Media Policy
Employees are a direct reflection of the business they work for. When writing your social media policy, address behavior expectancy – clearly outline who the policy holds accountable, where and how it needs to be upheld. Here are a few examples of what to include in your social media policy:

• Protecting business confidentiality
• Responsibility when interacting online as a business representative.
• The purpose of social media usage for your business and the goals you wish to achieve.
• Crediting information you share online.
• Highlighting the target audience with which you will engage with online.

A Social Media Policy for Financial Advisors
Please see the attached template in the Resources section in the back of this book.

Static vs. Interactive Content:
What's the Difference and Which is Better?

When it comes to social media and compliance for financial advisors, FINRA has different regulations depending on whether a social media post is *static* or *interactive*. If you're new to social media, don't let these definitions intimidate you! Here is a quick breakdown of the two forms of content, as well as what needs to be pre-approved and archived.

> "Think twice before you speak, because your words and influence will plant the seed of either success or failure in the mind of another."
>
> -Napoleon Hill

Static content is content that doesn't change. For example, your social media profile, photos, blog posts and websites are all considered to be *static* and must receive pre-approval by your firm's principal.

The other form of content is *interactive*, which includes Facebook status updates, tweets, LinkedIn updates and blog comments. *Interactive* content is created when you engage with others on social media and does not require prior approval. However, supervision and post-review are required. Additionally, no matter what device you post from, FINRA regulations state that all business-related social media content must be archived for a minimum of three years. Therefore, no matter what form of content advisors are creating online, both a social media policy and an archiving solution are vital to your firm's social media presence.

Now that the difference between the two types of content is clear, you may be wondering which form of content is better. *Interactive* content leads to engagement, keeping customers and prospects on your profile longer. Having all of the eyes on your social media site is a huge benefit of *interactive* content. Furthermore, if you are sharing and creating relevant content, social media users will have the opportunity to share, thus possibly increasing your search engine rankings. When creating *interactive* content, remember that it's about the customer's experience – understanding your customers needs in the financial industry and incorporating it into your online marketing strategy should be your top priority on social media.

Whenever I advise my clients to create a social media policy, they always respond with: *okay, but what should it say?* I understand because that was *my* first question when I first discovered the importance of a social media policy too. What should your social media policy include? How do you even get started?

5 Social Media Policy Tips for Financial Advisors

There are several different approaches you can take when creating a social media policy. Aim to make the policy specific and relevant to your firm. Also make sure it coincides with your compliance regulations. Here are a few simple steps to get you started in the writing process.

(1) First, Address the Purpose of Social Media
Why is your business using social media? Why are you crafting a social media policy? What should the reader/user take away after reading the policy? These are all important questions that need to be addressed in the introduction of your policy. In essence, you need to set the stage and make sure everyone is clear on the "why's."

(2) Define "Social Media"
Next is the "what." What is social media? Which social media platforms are your business a part of? Once again, this is important for laying the groundwork of your social media policy. Assume your readers aren't versed in social media.

(3) Personal Websites

Before you delve into the social media best practices of your business, establish guidelines for how employees (who identify themselves as an employee of your firm) should conduct and present themselves on their personal pages. In light of the assumption that employees are speaking on behalf of the organization, ensure that their communications are transparent, ethical and accurate. Also establish guidelines for how employees should engage with clients.

(4) Establish "Best Practices" for the Various Platforms

Establish general guidelines and best practices for the various social media platforms. How should your associates conduct themselves on social media? What are the compliance regulations set forth by FINRA and the SEC? Here are a few topics you may want to address:

- Images
- Commenting
- Posting
- Controversial issues
- Conflicts of interest
- Confidential information
- Responsibility, best judgment, ethics

Sharlyn Lauby of Mashable suggests "focusing on things that employees can rather than what they can't do." Why? Because social media is about leveraging the positive.

When creating this information remember the three S's of social media policies.

- **Simple**: Be a Hemingway. Use plain grammar and easily accessible language. If you use heavy jargon and technical terms, your readers are more likely to misunderstand things.

- **Short**: Your policy need not be a novel. Make it short, and to the point. Also make it navigable for the readers by using headers and bullet points.

- **Specific**: Back in May 2012, GM was accused of developing "unlawful" social media policies. According to the National Labor Relations Board (NLRB), the policies "infringed upon workers' rights by enforcing vague and overly stringent rules." For example, GM prohibited workers from posing anything "misleading" and urged employees to "think twice before friending colleagues." Given the vagueness of the policies, GM was allegedly "discouraging communications among co-workers." Prohibiting employees from posting anything "misleading," according to the NLRB, could be subject to lawful criticism of working conditions. Yikes! This situation offers a valuable lesson for your firm – especially considering the stringent regulations set forth by the SEC and FINRA. Be detailed. Don't use vague language.

(5) Protocols for Crisis Situations

Many companies fail to include this element in their social media policy. Let's face it: people are fallible—and it's better to prepare for crisis situations than get caught empty handed in a storm. The NatWest situation in the UK is a case-in-point example of why you should have a protocol for crisis situations.

Best Practices on Social Media

Social media profiles such as Facebook, LinkedIn and Twitter are online continuations of your brand. Therefore, when building your social media presence, take a moment to stop and reflect on the brand you want to establish and your firm's online goals. In order to be successful, consider how you want to be recognized in your market and what message you have to share with customers and prospects. Social media and branding go hand in hand – your profiles will allow you to connect with a huge pool of people and begin to build relationships. With all of the possibilities social media provides, it is crucial to brand your business effectively and consistently. This is where *static* content becomes extremely important to your brand's online image. To help you get started, here are 10 social media do's and don'ts:

Do's:

1. Do insure your biography, profile picture, website and other social media links are consistent across all social media platforms.
2. Do remember to be a good listener and learn from successful social media users you follow.
3. Do credit all sources before you share online.
4. Do share news and information about your business, firm members, and goals with your followers and connections on social media.
5. Do measure and monitor your social accounts and analytics on your content.

Don'ts:

6. Don't just be a commercial for your business – share engaging content that will interest your target market (even if the news is not about you).
7. Don't look at social media as a one way street – it requires engaging your followers and sharing quality content.
8. Don't lose sight of being professional when you are representing your identity and business brand online.
9. Don't forget to plan about audio, images and video, along with your text based content you share on social media.

10. Don't forget to establish a social media policy and archive your activity.

By keeping in mind these do's and don'ts, your firm can begin to brand itself positively online. Furthermore, feel free to adjust and add different do's and don'ts depending on your business' social media strategy. Online branding is one way that your marketing and compliance departments can build a relationship and collaborate on achieving a common goal.

"Compliance is tricky for those in the financial industry. I've figured out what they want and need. A lot of times it's me educating the compliance team. It is a lot of work at first, but then you can create systems and make it flow smoothly." Britney Castro, Financially Wise Women, @Brittneycastro

Social Media Archiving

The requirement to archive and retain records of all communication via social networks seems tedious, doesn't it? (Rules 17a-3 and 17a-4 under the Securities Exchange Act of 1934 and NASD Rule 3110). As restraining and "un-fun" as it sounds, there are some great archiving software and tools that not only do the work for you, but also offer distinct marketing advantages. Below are a few benchmarks to help you find a comprehensive social media archiving solution.

So, What Does Communication via Social Media Entail? Here are some examples of interactive content that must be archived.

- Blog posts
- Tweets
- Facebook status updates
- LinkedIn updates

- Comments
- Instant messaging
- Webinars

For more details, download the complimentary Financial Social Media Compliance Guide at http://financialsocialmedia .com/resources/compliance-guide.

How is Social Media Archiving Advantageous?

According to Arkovi, a social media archiving company, the right social media archiving solution goes beyond mere data retention. It can drive business development, discovery and make your marketing more effective in the following ways:

- Offers the ability to facilitate satisfying the compliance requirements to participate in social media.
- Supports the use of professional and personal systems and devices at any time.
- Integrates online monitoring of content from sources other than your social media content—this could include RSS feeds, Twitter searches, Google alerts, and more. You should be able to export them to an Excel spreadsheet for easy analysis and team collaboration.
- Offers the ability to view the results of compliance-driven monitoring and marketing-driven monitoring through a single dashboard—this is much more convenient than clicking through numerous emails and computer screens.
- Rich source for content ideas.
- Helps you see what content is getting the most feedback and attention.

What Archiving Platform Should I Use?

There is a medley of awesome social media archiving hubs for financial professionals. Here is a list of the top 6 to help you begin your search.

- **Arkovi**: Built in the cloud, Arkovi monitors and archives incoming and outgoing social media communications, including blogs, Facebook, LinkedIn, Twitter, websites and more. They deliver this across all devices —PC, Mac, and smartphones.

- **Actiance** : The Actiance platform provides granular security, management, and compliance features for unified communications (UC) and collaboration applications. Actiance's platform supports Microsoft Lync/OCS, IBM Sametime, IBM Connections, Cisco Unified Presence, public instant messaging (IM) platforms, industry-focused networks such as Reuters and Bloomberg, Web 2.0-enabled websites, blogs, wikis, webmail, and social media sites such as Facebook, LinkedIn, and Twitter. Content from these sources can be moderated, monitored, and archived – reducing outbound data leakage and enabling compliance with industry regulations, legal discovery requirements, and corporate policy standards.

- **Global Relay Archive**: Pre-review tools finally bring compliance officers into the approval queue mitigating the barriers to social media messaging for financial firms.

- **Hearsay**: Hearsay Social enables enterprises to engage with their customers via social media at every level of the organization—from brand to region to local stores, agents, or employees. Fortune 500 companies like Farmers Insurance Group use Hearsay Social to manage multiple corporate brand pages as well as over 5,000 local agent pages. Hearsay Social delivers enterprise-class scale, reliability, and regulatory compliance for financial services, insurance, retail, and other distributed organizations on Facebook, Twitter, LinkedIn, and Google+.

- **Erado**: Erado offers a full line of email, social media, instant message archiving, encryption, message security, and disaster recovery solutions designed for FINRA, SEC, Sarbanes-Oxley, Gramm-Leach-Bliley, FERC, NERC, and HIPAA compliance.

- **Socialware**: This platform is a comprehensive social business management solution that empowers financial services professionals to engage, acquire, and retain a higher volume of customers. Their three major products are Socialware Voices, Socialware, Socialware Insights.

- **Hootsuite**: HootSuite's new Enterprise archiving solution provides the most comprehensive social media dashboard and archiving combination in the industry. With HootSuite Social Compliance, clients can tap HootSuite Enterprise for social media engagement, collaboration, analytics, security and training while also managing the review and supervision of social media communications.

Listening — A Key Ingredient to Social Media Success
Listening is a central discipline to cultivate when engaging in social media. That counts for the beginner to the expert. Many social media users get ahead of themselves when posting content and creating profiles. However, what good is a social media profile if your target audience doesn't care what you have to say? That's precisely why a social media presence should begin with listening. Some of the most successful businesses have setup profiles, began following customers, prospects and influencers online and then just sat back and listened for awhile. They took the time to hear what topics were trending in the financial industry, what discussion topics were being tweeted and posted about online, and what was important to their target audience. Listening is your social media roadmap – it tells you what direction to head in and what topics to hit along the way.

No matter what business you are in, your customers want to be understood and their questions answered. Social media gives you the advantage — people share their opinions, concerns and experiences on social media more than anywhere else. Listening will give you the time to understand the needs of your customers and prospects and then react. Advisors can then use the research they discover to build an editorial calendar. Perhaps what your customers say online will inspire you to write a blog post or record a podcast. Remember, social media is all about engagement. Listening can be your secret weapon — find out what is relevant to your target audience and then address it and share it online. What's easier than that?

Furthermore, listening allows you to discover how people are talking about your services and their overall experience with you. While online, you can monitor what people are telling their friends and connections, but not necessarily telling you directly. Taking the time to listen provides you with the opportunity to measure your social media results and find out what you're doing right and what you're doing wrong. Advisors can then respond to these results by making easy changes while providing excellent customer service. Or, on the flip side, you can discover what people are saying about your competition. Learning from their success and mistakes can be a turning point in your business strategy and all you have to do is listen and use what you find to your advantage.

CHAPTER 10

TIMELESS PRINCIPLES

"The only way to make sense out of change is to plunge into it, move with it, and join the dance." – Alan Watts

As we approach the end of this book, your head should be filled with a whirlwind of ideas about how you can use social media in your business. So far, we've touched on a medley of topics and peppered in a lot of wisdom from some of the industry's leading experts. In this final chapter, I want to fuse all of this information together with some timeless gems that you can keep in your business toolbox for years to come.

Marketing is Nothing New

Marketing, sales, public relations, and relationship management are not new phenomenons. In fact, the concept of persuasion and marketing extends far back in history.

In feudal times, transactions came in the form of trade. Merchants strategically marketed their goods, labor, and services in order to reel in potential customers. Actors paraded in streets to persuade passersby to go to the theater. Wine sellers gave samples of their wine to entice people to buy. How else would they promote their service and survive?

After the industrial revolution and the development of the corporation, advertising often came in the form of brochures, signs, print ads, and then later, radio and television commercials. But more than static advertisements, word of mouth, networking, and referrals played a huge role in the growth of businesses. They don't call em' "mom and pop shops" for no reason. The hospitality, genuine care, and community that businesses fostered made it feel like customers were a part of a family, which prompted them to refer their friends and family.

Although times have changed, technology has evolved, and advertising has become more scientifically and psychologically sophisticated, the underlying principles of good business marketing still remain strong. It's not simply about selling a product or service, it's about enhancing the quality of life of those who come to you. It's about relationship building. It's about enhancing lives and guiding people to achieve their goals. If you keep this attitude, there will be a mutually fulfilling reciprocity.

Whether it's on social media or any other form of marketing, here are some timeless principles that you can employ to create success.

Passion
Your passion, or lack thereof *is* obvious. Despite what you perceive, your prospects and clients can sense your attitude, and will be more attracted to you if you genuinely care and

believe in what you're doing. Keep in mind that your leadership and energy is also infectious to your associates.

Integrity

Integrity in both internal and external areas of your business is essential for building a reputation that generates referrals. Stated simply: do what you say you're going to do, deliver exactly what you promise, and live as an example for what you teach.

Service and Customer Focus

In order to meet the needs of your clients and prospects, you must first understand exactly what their needs are. Not only their peripheral needs, but their personal needs also. What are some of the problems your audience experiences? What are their dreams and goals? What are their strengths and weaknesses? All of these points are important to consider when crafting your social media and online marketing strategies.

Trust

Do you ever go to Starbucks Coffee? If so, what do you order? My guess is that you probably order the same drink every time you go. Why? Because you know what you're getting. You know what to expect. Part of building trust is consistency. You must consistently deliver a service that goes above and beyond. Set high expectations for what your clients will achieve and experience with your service, and don't waver.

Relationships

Relationships are reciprocal in nature. They require both giving and receiving from the other party. By building tight relationships with those you work for and work with, you will set the foundation for a prosperous and trustworthy business. Social media provides the perfect space to do this. Share your life with others, and they will naturally share theirs with you.

"I think there is room for all advisors to be on social media. Even if they have compliance, they can still have personal Facebook and Twitter page. Having a presence on these platforms has lead me to many in-person relationships. I also believe it increases people's overall comfort level with you." -Brittney Castro, Financially Wise Women, @Brittneycastro

Whether you're a merchant that sells wine, or a financial advisor that gives investment and retirement advice, these timeless principles will win you loyal consumers. Whenever you approach a conundrum or stand-still in your marketing efforts, revisit these principles to help guide you.

Weaving it All Together

Assuming you've read this entire book, you should have a fairly solid grasp on what social media is all about. Independently, you should know how to maintain a compelling blog and generate a following on Facebook, Twitter, YouTube and LinkedIn. But the art of solidifying your social presence is in synergizing your networks. By that I mean creating cohesiveness between all of the platforms.

Have a Consistent Personality
If you have a light-hearted and goofy tone on one platform, and a more serious tone on another--it creates inconsistencies in your brand. Your audience will recognize this inconsistency--whether it's on a conscious or subconscious level. If you outsource your social media operations, make sure everyone understands the voice and personality of your brand.

Promote on All Networks
Strive to cross promote on all of your social media networks. For example, if you have a new follower on Twitter, thank them and ask them to come check out your Facebook page.

If you have a new connection on LinkedIn, ask them to follow you on Twitter.

You can also cross promote by using widgets to embed your blog into your LinkedIn and Facebook pages.

Don't Forget Social Media is a Two-Way Conversation

When it's all said and done, it's easy to forget that social media is about engaging. If you ever get to the point where you're simply blasting content without engaging with anyone else, take some time to sift through some posts and offer some genuine feedback.

Align Social Media to Your PR Activity

Have an upcoming book you're getting ready to publish? How about a client appreciation event that's coming up? Make sure your social media activity bolsters other initiative and ventures your business is taking.

Social media should play an integral role in all areas of your business. It is a part of the family, so to speak. So prepare to weave it into everything!

Learning from the Best

"In order to be the best, you must learn from the best" -Unknown

When it comes to achieving groundbreaking success in any area of life, there is almost always an element of learning that must take place. For instance, if you want to be a famous novelist, it is advisable to study the Hemingway's, Faulkner's, Throreau's, and Tolstoy's. If you long to be a famous musician, you'll unquestionably benefit from studying the Beethoven's, Steven Tyler's, and Pink Floyd's. Studying success helps you understand the science and art of achieving results.

In the social media world, the same principal applies. Many financial advisors want to have an impactful online presence, and in order to do so, it's necessary to research and to model after those who know what's up. Here are ten financial professionals that have established a strong social media presence and are worth modeling after.

The Financial Soldier, Jeff Rose: Jeff Rose, CFP®, is very keen on expressing his personality and background on social media. He creatively combines his military background, financial background, and passion for crossfit for an interesting social media package. He posts about financial topics and seeks to educate others on financial matters in an engaging and entertaining style. On some of his notable blog posts, he talks about savings and budgeting movements. His passion, creativity, and authenticity comes through in his blog, videos, and posts, and is worth modeling after.

- Twitter: @jjeffrose
- Blog/Website: www.goodfinancialcents.com
- Facebook: www.facebook.com/ GoodFinancialCents.JeffRose.CFP

The Social Butterfly, Brittney Castro: Brittney Castro, CFP®, is a social butterfly online. She excels in engaging in conversation with professionals and followers on social media. Similar to the other social media leaders, she frequently adds a personal touch to her tweets—be it commentary, fun facts, or memorable quotes. She is also very good about speaking to her target audience (women ages 30 to 40), and cross promoting her website and blog. Brittney is also a superstar on YouTube. Check out her channel to get great ideas on video content.

- Twitter: @brittneycastro
- Website: www.financiallywisewomen.com
- YouTube: www.youtube.com/user/brittneycastro
- Facebook: www.facebook.com/ FinanciallyWiseWomen

The Reporter, Jamie Cox: Jamie Cox embraces a relatively professional, serious voice on social media. You won't find crass or sass in his tweets, only expertise and proficiency. The information he tweets is very similar to the information that one would find in the NY Times—relevant topics, both domestic and international. He has undoubtedly established himself as a highly professional and credible financial source.

- Twitter: @jamesacoxiii
- Website/Blog: www.harrisfinancialgroup.com
- Facebook: www.facebook.com/HarrisFinancial Group

The Nerd, Michael Kitces: Self-proclaimed "financial nerd" Michael Kitces claims to provide a "nerd's perspective on the financial planning world." He offers a medley of information, ranging from relevant financial articles to technical graphs to thought-provoking quotes. On social media, he's established himself as a thoughtful, engaged resource for simplifying the complex nature of financial topics.

- Twitter: @MichaelKitces
- Website/Blog: www.kitces.com
- Facebook: www.facebook.com/pages/ Kitcescom/135174283225230

The Witty Financial Expert, Josh Brown: Josh Brown is well known for his sarcastic, witty, and amusing social personality. On his networks, he strikes a unique balance between being informative and entertaining. He blasts out a mix of information, ranging from the politics and economics to the Olympic games. In his website, he claims, "I'll use statistics, satire, anecdotes, pop culture references, sarcasm, fact, fantasy and any other device that I feel necessary to get my points across." And that is exactly what he does!

- Twitter: @ReformedBroker
- Website/Blog: www.thereformedbroker.com
- Facebook: www.facebook.com/StockTwits

The Committed Investment Advisor, Bryan Weiss: Bryan Weiss is very passionate about providing solid education and advice about investment planning. On his blog and social media platforms, he specifically speaks to investors and offers a lot of valuable information about investing. His success comes from honing in on a specific financial topic. If people are in interested solely in investment related

topics, his social media platforms are the place to be.
- Twitter: @MarianFinancial
- Website/Blog: blog.marianfinancial.com
- Facebook: www.facebook.com/MarianFinacial Partners/
- YouTube: www.youtube.com/marianfinancial

 **Main Street Money Hero, Mark Matson:** Mark Matson is a prominent figure in the financial industry. On his Twitter bio, this is how he describes himself and his career: "Manages 3.2 billion dollars, financial guru, CNBC and Fox Business guest, Bloomberg, Host – Matson Money Live, internet investing and news show." It goes without question that he is a trusted and acclaimed resource in the financial world. On his social media platforms, he does a great job of striking a balance between personal and professional content. He posts about the economy, small business, politics, investing, with personal touches weaved in like photos of his family and office. Also, if you are interested in how you can establish a strong YouTube presence, use his channel as a springboard for ideas.
- Twitter: @MarkMatson
- Website/Blog: www.matsonmoney.com
- Facebook: www.facebook.com/MatsonMoney
- YouTube: www.youtube.com/markmatsontv

The Angry Capitalist, Dan Cuprill: On his social media platforms, Dan Cuprill takes a strong, supportive stance on free markets. His mission, according to his platforms, is to debunk the myths of investing promoted by Wall Street & the Financial Press. His tone tends to be firm, direct, and politically charged. For members of this school of thought, he is a valuable resource. Like Matson, he posts about politics, the economy, the matters relating to the financial industry. He is a great model of what it means to have a consistent personality and tone on all of his platforms.

- Twitter: DanCuprill
- Website/Blog: www.dancuprill.com
- Facebook: www.facebook.com/matsonandcuprill

Stephanie Holmes, The Money Finder: Stephanie Holmes is an author, speaker, columnist, and financial advisor. On her website, she considers herself a passionate crusader who would have all financial advisors not only help their clients with investments but also debt and spending to create true wealth. On her platforms, she embodies this mission with gusto. In addition to blasting out financial information, she also peppers in snippets of her personal life--like being a mother and a wife. She is great at balance, creativity, and inspiring others through her social presence.

- Twitter: @themoneyfinder:
- Website/Blog: themoneyfinder.ca
- Facebook: www.facebook.com/themoneyfinder.ca

Michelle Matson, Dressed to Invest: Michelle Matson is a great resource for women in the financial industry. From financial advice to beauty and fitness tips, she has pioneered a niche audience on social media. As Vice President at Matson Money, she continues to develop training tools, educational materials and programs for investors and financial advisors. She extends this expertise on social media by offering unique and valuable information to her audience.

- Twitter: @MichelleMatson
- Website/Blog: www.michellematson.com
- Facebook: www.facebook.com/DressedToInvest

These financial professionals are the cream of the crop when it comes to social media. If you are ever unsure of how to approach social media, visit their platforms for some creative inspiration.

ENDNOTES

Preface
- Guy Kawasaki. The Art of Communication

Chapter 1
- Marshall Rosenberg. Non-Violent Communication
- Facebook Newsroom.
  http://newsroom.fb.com/content/default.aspx?NewsAreaId=22
- Socialnomics.com
  http://www.socialnomics.net/2012/06/06/10-new-2012-social-media-stats-wow/
- YouTube Statistics
  http://www.youtube.com/t/press_statistics
- Chris Katterjohn, Chris Burnes, and Colin Vaughan. Indianapolis Business Journal.
  http://www.slideshare.net/james.burnes/how-obama-won-using-digital-and-social-media-presentation
- Jeff Loucks, Robert Waitman, and Jörgen Ericsson . Winning the Battle for the Wealthy Investor. New Cisco IBSG Study Uncovers Significant Opportunity To Address Needs of Wealthy Under-50 Investors
- Spectrem Group. "Wealthy Young Investors."
  http://www.spectrem.com/reports/wealthy-young-investors-114
- Social Media Today. "How Fortune 500 Use Social Media 2012."
  http://socialmediatoday.com/martinmeyergossner/490826/how-fortune-500-use-social-media-2012
- Financial Advisor Magazine. "Social Media Losing Some Appeal with Financial Advisors."
  http://www.fa-mag.com/component/content/article/9809.html?issue=185&magazineID=1&Itemid=73

Chapter 2
- Dale Carnegie. "How to Win Friends and Influence People."

Chapter 3
- Erik Qualman, Digital Leader
- Financial Planning. "A Look Inside LPL Financial's Social Media Strategy." http://www.financial-planning.com/news/lpl-financial-social-media-strategy-2674766-1.html?zkPrintable =1&nopagination=1

Chapter 4:
- Tech Crunch. "Start Up School: Interview with Mark Zuckerberg." http://techcrunch.com/2009/10/24/startup-school-an-interview-with-mark-zuckerberg/
- The Daily Mail. http://www.dailymail.co.uk/news/article-2184658/Is-joining-Facebook-sign-youre-psychopath-Some-employers-psychologists-say-suspicious.html
- Inside Facebook http://www.insidefacebook.com/2009/02/02/fastest-growing-demographic-on-facebook-women-over-55/

Chapter 5: Blogging
- Coker, Brent http://www.webreep.com/blog/post/2011/11/14/What-makes-a-30-second-movie-go-viral.aspx

Chapter 6: Twitter
- CNNTech
  http://articles.cnn.com/2011-11-02/tech/tech_social-media_twitter-stories_1_hashtag-tweets-twitter-critics?_s=PM:TECH
- Wikipedia
  http://en.wikipedia.org/wiki/April_25%E2%80%9328,_2011_tornado_outbreak
  http://en.wikipedia.org/wiki/Twitter

Chapter 7: LinkedIn
- Social Media Times
  http://socialtimes.com/survey-49-of-linkedin-users-have-household-income-over-100k_b87449
- Social Media Sonar
  http://socialmediasonar.com/the-four-linkedin-connection-strategies
- LinkedIn Blog
  http://blog.linkedin.com/2008/12/05/jeff-ragovin-buddy-media/
- Linkedin Marketing, "Device and Demand: How LinkedIn Members are Driving for Consumer Electronic Devices."
  http://marketing.linkedin.com/sites/default/files/pdfs/Infographic_LinkedIn_CE_US_2012.pdf

Chapter 8: YouTube
- YouTube
  http://www.youtube.com/watch?v=W4nD6y-PnUY&feature=relmfu
  http://www.youtube.com/watch?v=B6kbHR4O3JU&fmt=18]
- Social Media Today. "Maximizing Video SEO Tips and Tricks You Should Know".
  http://socialmediatoday.com/tom-bishop/514640/maximizing-video-seo-tips-and-tricks-you-should-know

Chapter 9: Compliance

- FINRA Regulatory Notice 10-06
  http://www.finra.org/web/groups/industry/@ip/@
  reg/@notice/documents/notices/p120779.pdf
- FINRA Regulatory Notice 11-36
  http://www.finra.org/web/groups/industry/@ip/@
  reg/@notice/documents/notices/p124186.pdf
- SEC National Examination Risk Alert
  http://www.sec.gov/about/offices/ocie/riskalert-
  socialmedia.pdf
- Financial Social Media Compliance Guide
  http://www.financialsocialmedia.com/compliance-
  guide-pd

RESOURCES

FINANCIAL SOCIAL MEDIA
DAILY CHECKLIST

Twitter

	SHARE	STATUS
	Post 2 Tweets w/content	
.	Include links	
.	Schedule out	
.	RSS Feeds	
	UPDATE STATUS	**STATUS**
	3 Re-Tweets	
.	Add commentary	
.	Add RT & hashtags	
	COMMENT	**STATUS**
	Quote, opinion or news	
.	Questions!	
.	@replies, @mentions, #hashtags	
	Interact	**STATUS**
.	Chat with 2 new connections	
.	Chat with 2 existing connections	
.	Constantly manage	

Facebook

	SHARE	STATUS

	1-2 posts with content
	    . Include links
	    . Include commentary
	    . Include photo or video	

	UPDATE STATUS	STATUS

	Quote, opinion or news
	    . Questions!
	    . Tagging	

	COMMENT	STATUS

	. News & current pages
	  . Comment on posts & updates
	  . Answer questions	

	Interact	STATUS

	. Constantly manage
	  . Give thanks
	  . Tagging	

LinkedIn

	SHARE	STATUS

	1-2 posts with content
	    . Include links
	    . Include commentary
	    . Include photo or video	

	UPDATE STATUS	STATUS
	. Quote, opinion or news . Questions!	
	COMMENT	STATUS

	. New & current groups
	      Comment on posts & updates
	      Answer questions	

	Interact	STATUS

	. Constantly manage
	  . Give thanks
	  . Group management	

SOCIAL MEDIA POLICY TEMPLATE

This document is provided freely as a service of Arkovi Social Media Archiving. You may use it as a model for structuring your social media policy as a Registered Investment Advisor.

We present it as guidance and not as professional legal advice. While our team has significant expertise in financial services across compliance, technology and operations – we highly recommend you consult your legal counsel during the process of developing your formal social media policy.

We can be contacted:
Arkovi
137 East Iron Avenue, 2nd Floor
Dover, OH 44622
1.866.222.2334
info@bmrw.com
http://www.arkovi.com

Proposed Policy Template

It is the policy of _____ investment adviser to allow its IARs to maintain social media accounts consisting of personal blogs and LinkedIn, Twitter and Facebook accounts subject to the following policies relating to their permitted usage of such accounts.

Additional social and web accounts are also permitted at the following sites and/or networks:

1. Add name and web address here
2. Add name and web address here
3. Add name and web address here
4. Add more as needed

To meet its supervisory obligations _____ investment adviser requires all of its corporate social media accounts to be loaded into the firm's social media archival system.

In addition, each investment adviser representative who uses social media shall:

1. a. Notify _____ investment adviser in writing of their existing and any new social media accounts or blogs he/she may have or wishes to open;
2. I personally have _____ blogs and or _____ social media accounts.
3. Provide _____ investment adviser with the name of the account for input into the archival system;
4. Sign an authorization, giving _____ investment adviser authority to monitor the account for purposes of its supervisory obligations; and
5. Maintain a copy of the _____ investment adviser CCO's written approval for each social media account he/she has opened.
6. On an annual basis, sign an attestation that all social media accounts or blogs he/she has used during the prior year have been previously reported to _____ investment adviser and if one or more are no longer in use, a statement to that effect.

Social media policies for investment adviser representatives are in most cases similar to if not identical to the investment advisor's pre-existing considerations with respect to its advertising policies under 206 (4)-1. Although not exclusively limited to the following suggestions, advisory social media policies should generally:

1. Prohibit posting of or linking to comments or content that is harassing, defamatory, indecent or misrepresents the stated policies, practices, performance returns or investment strategies provided by XYZ investment advisors.
2. Be honest and consistent with prior professional comments the IAR has provided to clients while providing investment advisory services or in presentations previously made on behalf of the firm.
3. Not include IAR comments that are in retaliation to negative posts or comments received on the IAR's site. If warranted, the IAR should work through the compliance department to address any issues that directly relate to customer issues identified in such posts.

4. Prohibit the acceptance of third party testimonials or recommendations, if the IAR has mentioned or otherwise indicated that he/she provides investment services on the social media site. While a testimonial as to the IAR's character may or may not be allowable, the *SEC has not as yet given any leeway to the general prohibition against the use of testimonials by investment advisory professionals*, at least if the communication is considered an advertisement. While the IAR cannot delete previously accepted testimonials, it is possible to block them from view. If the IAR has previously accepted a testimonial, he/she should go into their social media site and follow the steps to block from view any testimonials that he/she currently may have. Failure to reject or block previously accepted testimonials might subject the IAR to the investment adviser placing restrictions on the IAR's future social media usage or to possible disciplinary sanctions.

5. Prohibit the IAR's use of the "like" feature on the social media sites of others or from re-tweeting materials unless the investment adviser is fully comfortable with accepting the information that the IAR "liked" or "re-tweeted" as their own. If at all possible, the IAR should disable the like button on their site or blog and remove any instances where someone indicated liking material on these sites as soon as possible. Third party use of the like button could easily be considered an implied testimonial and thus would be prohibited under Rule 206.

6. Not include any favorable comment on the IAR's social media posts or blogs from themselves through other social media accounts the IAR may have.

7. Protect the customer's privacy by prohibiting the use of a customer's name address, identification information, financial, account holdings or any other information specific to a customer on the IAR's social media site.

8. Prohibit the IAR from using Facebook Chat 1.

9. Require any IAR who is also a registered representative to notify their broker dealer prior to making any LinkedIn or other social media profile change or other change that would be considered to be static content for pre-approval or content that would be considered sales literature prior to implementing the change on their social media site.

10. Prohibit IARs from providing legal or tax opinions or making specific investment recommendations on their social media site.

11. Prohibit the IAR from making any negative references about the investment adviser on his/her social media site, or from making any misrepresentation as to his/her title, responsibilities or function with the adviser.

12. Require the IAR to refrain from using superlatives, exaggeration or anything that might suggest a guaranteed return or guaranteed successful results.
13. Require the IAR to refrain from the use of industry jargon, consider his/her audience and prepare any posted materials so that his/her least sophisticated customer can clearly understand them.
14. Prohibit the use of a chart, graph, formula or other tool on the IAR's social media site that to be used in determining which securities to buy or sell or when to do so.
15. Require the IAR to follow standard performance guidelines in presenting adviser performance including the requirement to show returns net of applicable advisory fees and other required charges on the account.
16. Not offer any report, service, or analysis labeled as free on the IAR's social media site or blog unless it is in fact free with no further obligation or commitment.
17. Not disclose any material non public information in the IAR's possession
18. Not discuss or disclose the firm's proprietary information, intellectual property interests or other trade secrets on their social media site.
19. Use appropriate disclosures as to the IAR's business affiliations, relevant conflicts of interest and correctly attribute ownership of any comments, statements or quotes to their originator.
20. Prohibit any reference to past specific successful recommendations of securities, unless, the IAR provides a separate detailed list of all past recommendations good or bad over at least the past year, with the name of the security, the date recommended, and the price at which it was recommended. The IAR needs to include a legend that past performance is not an indication of future performance with the materials. This limits the IAR or the investment adviser from advertising past success, unless it is fairly presented. The IAR also needs to disclose all material facts relating to any recommendation. IAR posts as advertisements must not have any untrue statement of material fact or otherwise be false or misleading

RESOURCES

Books and Records

While it is unclear whether all social media should be considered an advertisement and as such required information to be maintained for a minimum of five (5) years, as a best practice, the investment adviser should probably capture any social media content that relates at all to the firm, whether it be in the form of a mention, a contact, a marketing blurb, a blog, a performance report, a tweet or re-tweet, a Facebook fan page or wall, a LinkedIn profile or otherwise.

While early efforts to comply with the provisions for maintenance of social media content have attempted to us hard copy reproductions of profiles, sites and comments as documentation, supervision under this type of process is virtually impossible to perform. The investment adviser is not easily able to verify whether the investment adviser has received all of the content and because the adviser doesn't have mediation capability, the adviser is unable to compare the hard copies to all of the activity in a social media account.

Advertising:

- Any communications to more than one person.
- Pre-approval of static posts to a social media site is not a regulatory requirement under the Advisors Act, unless required under the firm's policy.
- No specific formal archival process is mandated for maintenance and mediation of social media but as with email, the SEC and the states expect one.

RESOURCES

Supervisory policies

The _____ investment adviser will periodically monitor the social media archive through use of mediation software to identify any instances of misuse with respect to the requirements above. Should inappropriate comments or materials be found on an IAR's social media site, an in-depth review of the IAR's other social media content will be conducted. Action to be taken by the investment adviser shall be dependent on the results of the investigation and may include:

a) Remedial training on investment advisor advertising and the advisor's social media policies.
b) Prohibiting the IAR from any future use of the social media site.
c) Suspension or termination of employment as an IAR.

Code of Ethics

The investment adviser may if it so chooses include specific standards for IAR usage of social media under its investment adviser Code of Ethics. Although not a mandatory COE provision, many of the specific investment advisory policies relating to social media usage are consistent with ethical conduct and would be valid as conditions under the IAR's annual Code of Ethics attestation.

By specifically including some of the requirements for social media communications under its Code of Ethics, the investment adviser will have the ability to require the IAR to acknowledge an understanding of the policies under the Code and report any Code violations they become aware of which helps the investment adviser with its oversight function.

Please see the example forms templates for documenting approval for the use of social media and acceptance of policy guidelines by individual employees and/or additional individuals.

SOCIAL MEDIA ACCOUNT APPROVAL

As CCO of _____ investment adviser, I hereby approve

_____ to use the fol-
lowing personal blogs or social media accounts whether for his/her personal promotion of the advisor's investment advisory services or otherwise, subject to compliance with the advisor's policies for use of social
media.

_____,

_____,

_____,

_____,

_____

_____

SIGNATURE

_____

PRINTED NAME & TITLE

_____

Date

INVESTMENT ADVISER REPRESENTATIVE SOCIAL MEDIA AC-COUNT REVIEW AUTHORIZATION

I _____, as a in-vestment adviser representative with

_____ investment adviser, author-ize _____ investment adviser access to all blogs and/or social media accounts that I have previously disclosed or will open and disclose in the future for purposes of their regulatory supervisory responsibilities and recordkeeping.

By signing this authorization, I acknowledge that I have no expectations of privacy with respect to comments, posts or other communications that may be found on my blogs or social media sites. I agree to abide by all social media policies and procedures as implemented by _____, and acknowledge that my right to use these social media accounts is contingent on my compliance with these policies and procedures.

_____,

Signature

_____,

Printed Name

_____

Date

ACKNOWLEDGEMENTS

Everything we do at Financial Social Media is a team effort and this book is no exception. I am so thankful to have the support of such a smart, passionate group of innovative people who love what they do.

I'd like to extend a tremendous amount of gratitude and praise toward Amy Smith, who contributed significantly to the content development and research. You continue to amaze me, Amy, and it's been so exciting to watch your career develop. The sky is the limit for you! To Katie Malone, for her sharp design and creative ideas. To Heidi Williams, an amazing friend, talented designer, and loyal supporter of all my crazy endeavors for over a decade. To my family, for all of their love and support. To the rest of the team at Financial Social Media—thank you for all your support and awesomeness!

A special thank you to Blane Warrene with Arkovi, who is one of the most knowledgeable experts on compliance and social media strategy that I know. Your contribution is much appreciated!

And last, but certainly not least, to the amazing advisors who are pioneering the path to success in social media. Mark Matson, Brittney Castro, Jamie Cox, Michelle Matson, Michael Ham, Dan Cuprill, Josh Brown, Jeff Rose, Michael Kitces, Bryan Weiss, Stephanie Holmes, Chris Storace--thank you for all you do. You guys rock!

ABOUT AMY MCILWAIN

Entrepreneur, author, speaker, and worldwide connector, Amy McIlwain is internationally recognized for radical new ways of approaching social media, PR, marketing, advertising, and customer service within the financial service industry.

Amy has appeared live on NBC, CBS and FOX as a social media expert. Her content has been featured in several top financial industry publications, media outlets, blogs, books, and websites including the Wall Street Journal, Financial Times, InvestmentNews, AdvisorOne, ProducersWeb, Ignites, FundFire and more.

Described as "captivating", "insightful", and "an online marketing expert" it is no wonder Amy McIlwain is one of the most in-demand speakers in the financial industry. Her content-packed webinars and live trainings tackle the complex compliance issues within the financial industry and provide take-away's that yield immediate results.

@amymcilwain
www.amymcilwain.com
www.facebook.com/socialamy
www.youtube.com/amymcilwain
www.linkedin.com/in/amymcilwain

800.837.6330